Christmas
COOKING

THE AUSTRALIAN Women's Weekly

There's nothing in life I love more than good food, a festive occasion, family and friends (that's not necessarily in order of preference!), which is probably why Christmas is so special for so many of us. While preparing this book, it was exciting to put a special spin on some of our favourite traditional recipes, as well as develop new recipes, which may well become tomorrow's classics. Best of all, there's nothing daunting within these pages, so you'll be able to join your family and friends in having a very merry Christmas!

Pamela Clark

Food Director

CONTENTS

DRINKS   4

STARTERS   8

MAINS   24

VEGETABLES & SALADS   52

LEFTOVERS   66

DESSERTS   70

CAKES & PUDDINGS   82

CHRISTMAS GIFTS   102

COOKING TECHNIQUES   112

GLOSSARY   116

INDEX   118

FACTS & FIGURES   119

CHAMPAGNE COCKTAIL

PREPARATION TIME 5 MINUTES

Use marginally less than ⅔ cup of champagne for each cocktail and you will be able to make five cocktails from one bottle of champagne.

5cm strip orange rind
1 sugar cube
5 drops Angostura bitters
⅔ cup (160ml) chilled champagne

1 Slice rind thinly.
2 Place sugar cube in champagne glass; top with bitters then champagne. Garnish with rind.

serves 1

PARTY PUNCH

PREPARATION TIME 5 MINUTES (PLUS REFRIGERATION TIME)

We used a traminer riesling for this recipe.

2 x 750ml bottles chilled medium-dry white wine
1 tablespoon dark rum
⅓ cup (80ml) peach schnapps
2 tablespoons triple sec
1½ cups (375ml) apple and mandarin juice
3 star fruit (450g), sliced thickly
4 small peaches (460g), sliced thickly

1 Combine wine, rum, schnapps, triple sec and juice in large bowl. Stir in sliced fruit.
2 Refrigerate, covered, 1 hour before serving.

serves 8

AUSTRALIAN ICED TEA

PREPARATION TIME 5 MINUTES

3 teaspoons chilled sugar syrup (see recipe page 7)
3 teaspoons vodka
3 teaspoons white rum
3 teaspoons white tequila
2 teaspoons Cointreau
3 teaspoons gin
3 teaspoons lime juice
6 ice cubes
⅓ cup crushed ice
⅓ cup (80ml) chilled ginger beer
lime wedge, for garnish

1 Combine syrup, vodka, rum, tequila, Cointreau,
   gin, juice and ice cubes in cocktail shaker;
   shake vigorously.
2 Place crushed ice in cocktail glass; strain cocktail
   mixture over ice. Top with ginger beer; garnish
   with lime.

serves 1

MANGO DAIQUIRI

PREPARATION TIME 5 MINUTES

1 medium mango (430g), chopped coarsely
1 tablespoon lime juice
2 teaspoons Cointreau
1 tablespoon mango liqueur
¼ cup (60ml) white rum
½ cup crushed ice
lime slice, for garnish

1 Blend or process mango, juice, Cointreau, liqueur,
   rum and ice until just combined.
2 Pour into cocktail glass; garnish with lime.

serves 1

BELLINI

PREPARATION TIME 5 MINUTES

Originally made in Harry's Bar in Venice with prosecco, the region's sparkling wine, a bellini is just as moreish when made with champagne. Use white peaches instead of yellow, if in season.

2 medium peaches (300g), chopped coarsely
½ cup (125ml) peach schnapps
750ml chilled champagne
8 sugar cubes

1 Blend or process peach and schnapps until smooth. Combine peach mixture with champagne in large jug.
2 Place one sugar cube in each of eight champagne glasses; top with bellini mixture.

serves 8

DRUNKEN WATERMELON

PREPARATION TIME 30 MINUTES
(PLUS STANDING AND FREEZING TIME)

1 cup (250ml) vodka
½ cup (125ml) lime juice
½ cup (110g) caster sugar
¾ cup coarsely chopped fresh mint
1 seedless watermelon (3kg), halved
2 cups (500ml) chilled lemonade

1 Combine vodka, juice, sugar and mint in medium bowl; stand 1 hour.
2 Pierce melon flesh several times, taking care not to puncture outer skin. Strain vodka mixture into jug; pour half of it, gradually, over melon flesh. Enclose melon halves separately in plastic wrap; freeze overnight.
3 Remove melon from freezer; stand at room temperature 1 hour. Remove skin; chop melon coarsely.
4 Blend or process melon with remaining vodka mixture, in batches; pour each batch into punch bowl. Stir in lemonade.

makes 3 litres

LIME AND MINT SPRITZER

PREPARATION TIME 5 MINUTES
(PLUS REFRIGERATION TIME)
COOKING TIME 5 MINUTES

1 cup (250ml) lime juice
1.25 litres (5 cups) chilled mineral water
¼ cup coarsely chopped fresh mint

SUGAR SYRUP

½ cup (125ml) water
½ cup (110g) caster sugar

1 Make sugar syrup.
2 Combine syrup in large jug with juice, mineral water and mint. Serve immediately, with ice if desired.

SUGAR SYRUP Combine ingredients in small saucepan; stir over heat until sugar dissolves. Bring to a boil, remove from heat; refrigerate until cold.

serves 8

MIXED BERRY PUNCH

PREPARATION TIME 15 MINUTES
(PLUS REFRIGERATION TIME)

1 teabag
1 cup (250ml) boiling water
120g raspberries
150g blueberries
125g strawberries, halved
¼ cup loosely packed fresh mint leaves
750ml chilled sparkling apple cider
2½ cups (625ml) chilled lemonade

1 Place teabag in mug, cover with the boiling water; stand 10 minutes. Squeeze teabag over mug, discard teabag; cool tea 10 minutes.
2 Using fork, crush raspberries in punch bowl; add blueberries, strawberries, mint and tea. Stir to combine, cover; refrigerate 1 hour. Stir cider and lemonade into punch just before serving; sprinkle with extra mint leaves, if desired.

serves 8

TOMATO, LEEK AND MARINATED FETTA TARTLETS

PREPARATION TIME 45 MINUTES (PLUS REFRIGERATION TIME)
COOKING TIME 35 MINUTES

1 medium leek (350g)
20g butter
1 tablespoon olive oil
2 sheets ready-rolled puff pastry
250g cherry tomatoes, sliced thinly
½ teaspoon fresh thyme leaves
1 tablespoon red wine vinegar

MARINATED FETTA

1 teaspoon finely grated lemon rind
¼ teaspoon cracked black pepper
2 cloves garlic, crushed
2 teaspoons fresh thyme leaves
200g fetta cheese, cut into 24 pieces
1¼ cups (310ml) olive oil

1 Make marinated fetta.
2 Preheat oven to hot.
3 Cut leek into 6cm pieces; cut pieces in half lengthways, slice halves lengthways into thin strips. Heat butter and oil in large frying pan; cook leek, stirring occasionally, about 20 minutes or until soft.
4 Meanwhile, cut each pastry sheet into twelve 6cm x 8cm rectangles; place on lightly oiled oven trays. Fold in each side to form a 2mm border; prick pastry pieces with fork. Bake, uncovered, in hot oven about 10 minutes or until browned lightly. Remove from oven; using fork, immediately press pastry pieces down to flatten. Reduce oven temperature to moderately hot.
5 Meanwhile, place tomato in medium bowl with thyme and vinegar; toss gently to combine.
6 Spread 1 tablespoon of the leek mixture over each pastry piece; crumble one piece of the cheese over each then top with tomato mixture. Bake, uncovered, in moderately hot oven about 5 minutes or until tomato just softens. Serve immediately.

MARINATED FETTA Combine rind, pepper, garlic and thyme in medium sterilised glass jar having a tight-fitting lid; add cheese. Seal jar then shake gently to coat cheese in mixture. Open jar and pour in enough of the oil to completely cover cheese mixture. Reseal; refrigerate overnight.

makes 24

TIPS The fetta can be marinated up to two weeks before making the tartlets; keep, covered, under refrigeration.
Work with one puff pastry sheet at a time, keeping the other in the freezer so that it doesn't become too soft.

RACLETTE PARCELS IN VINE LEAVES AND PROSCIUTTO

PREPARATION TIME 25 MINUTES COOKING TIME 5 MINUTES

If you cannot find raclette, you can substitute it with gruyère, appenzeller or even emmentaler. Grapevine leaves, available in cans or cryovac-packed in brine, can be found in Greek and Middle Eastern food stores as well as most delicatessens.

2 tablespoons finely chopped
 fresh basil
1 fresh small red thai chilli,
 chopped finely
2 teaspoons finely grated
 lemon rind
1 tablespoon lemon juice
2 teaspoons olive oil
500g piece raclette cheese,
 cut into 24 pieces
8 slices prosciutto (120g)
24 grapevine leaves in brine,
 rinsed, drained

1 Place basil, chilli, rind, juice and oil in medium bowl with cheese; toss gently to combine. Cut each prosciutto slice lengthways into three even strips.
2 Centre one cheese piece on each vine leaf; fold leaf over cheese to enclose completely. Wrap one strip of prosciutto around each vine-leaf parcel.
3 Heat large non-stick frying pan; cook parcels, uncovered, about 5 minutes or until prosciutto is crisp all over.

makes 24

MINI SCALLOP AND LIME KEBABS

PREPARATION TIME 15 MINUTES (PLUS REFRIGERATION TIME) **COOKING TIME** 5 MINUTES

2 tablespoons vegetable oil
4cm piece fresh ginger
    (20g), grated
3 cloves garlic, crushed
24 scallops (600g), roe removed
3 limes
12 fresh kaffir lime leaves,
    halved lengthways
24 sturdy toothpicks

1 Combine oil, ginger and garlic in
   medium bowl, add scallops; toss
   scallops to coat in marinade.
   Cover; refrigerate 30 minutes.
2 Meanwhile, cut each lime into
   eight wedges. Skewer one piece
   of lime leaf and one lime wedge
   onto each toothpick.
3 Cook scallops on oiled grill
   plate (or grill or barbecue) about
   5 minutes or until cooked as
   desired. Stand 5 minutes then
   skewer one onto each toothpick.

makes 24

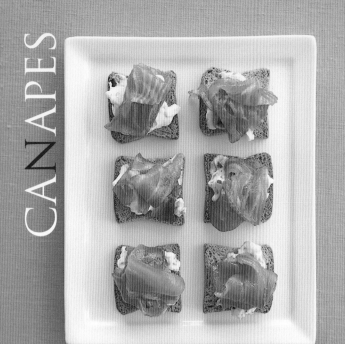

VODKA-CURED GRAVLAX

PREPARATION TIME 10 MINUTES
(PLUS REFRIGERATION TIME)

1 tablespoon sea salt
1 teaspoon finely ground black pepper
1 tablespoon sugar
1 tablespoon vodka
300g salmon fillet, skin on
24 melba toasts

SOUR CREAM SAUCE

⅓ cup (80g) sour cream
2 teaspoons drained baby capers, rinsed
2 teaspoons lemon juice
2 teaspoons finely chopped drained cornichons
½ small red onion (50g), chopped finely

1 Combine salt, pepper, sugar and vodka in small bowl.
2 Remove bones from fish; place fish, skin-side down, on piece of plastic wrap. Spread vodka mixture over flesh side of fish; enclose securely in plastic wrap. Refrigerate overnight, turning parcel several times.
3 Make sour cream sauce.
4 Slice fish thinly; spread sauce on toasts, top with fish.

SOUR CREAM SAUCE Combine ingredients in small bowl.

makes 24

FIG AND FETTA

PREPARATION TIME 10 MINUTES

You can either purchase marinated fetta at your favourite delicatessen or make your own (see our recipe on page 8).

125g marinated fetta cheese
1 tablespoon finely chopped fresh chives
24 melba toasts
3 medium fresh figs (180g)

1 Using fork, mash cheese with chives in small bowl; spread on one side of each toast.
2 Cut each fig into eight wedges; place one wedge on each toast. Sprinkle with coarsely ground black pepper, if desired.

makes 24

MUSTARD BEEF

PREPARATION TIME 10 MINUTES
COOKING TIME 5 MINUTES

2 tablespoons wholegrain mustard
2 tablespoons horseradish cream
2 new york-cut steaks (440g)
2 teaspoons olive oil
¼ cup (60g) sour cream
24 baby spinach leaves (50g)

CROSTINI

1 small french bread stick
olive-oil spray

1 Combine half of the mustard and half of
   the horseradish in small bowl; spread over
   steaks. Refrigerate, covered, until required.
2 Make crostini.
3 Heat oil in large frying pan; cook steaks,
   uncovered, until cooked as desired. Cover;
   stand 5 minutes then slice thinly.
4 Combine remaining mustard and remaining
   horseradish with sour cream in small bowl.
   Top crostini with spinach, steak slices and
   sour cream mixture.

CROSTINI Preheat oven to moderately slow.
Discard ends of bread; cut into 1cm slices. Place
slices, in single layer, on oven tray; spray with oil.
Toast, both sides, in moderately slow oven.

makes 24

DUCK AND HOISIN CROSTINI

PREPARATION TIME 15 MINUTES
(PLUS REFRIGERATION TIME)
COOKING TIME 15 MINUTES

2 green onions
2 cups (250g) thinly sliced barbecued duck meat
½ lebanese cucumber (65g), seeded, sliced thinly
¼ cup (60ml) hoisin sauce

CROSTINI

1 small french bread stick
olive-oil spray

1 Make crostini.
2 Meanwhile, cut green stem part of onions into
   8cm pieces; slice each piece lengthways into
   12 thin strips (reserve white bulb sections of onions
   for another use). Place green onion strips in small
   bowl of iced water; refrigerate about 20 minutes
   or until curled.
3 Top crostini with duck, cucumber, sauce and
   onion curl.

CROSTINI Preheat oven to moderately slow.
Discard ends of bread; cut into 1cm slices. Place
slices, in single layer, on oven tray; spray with oil.
Toast, both sides, in moderately slow oven.

makes 24

YABBIES WITH REMOULADE ON BAGUETTE

PREPARATION TIME 50 MINUTES **COOKING TIME** 5 MINUTES

24 small uncooked yabbies (1.5kg)
1 medium lemon (140g), sliced thickly
1 tablespoon finely chopped
   fresh chives
2 teaspoons finely grated lemon rind
1 tablespoon lemon juice
1 small french bread stick

REMOULADE
2 egg yolks
2 teaspoons white wine vinegar
2 teaspoons wholegrain mustard
2 tablespoons water
1¼ cups (310ml) vegetable oil
1 tablespoon drained capers,
   rinsed, chopped finely
1 tablespoon finely chopped fresh dill

1 Bring large saucepan of water to a boil,
   add yabbies and sliced lemon; cook,
   uncovered, about 5 minutes or until
   yabbies are changed in colour. Drain;
   discard lemon and cooking liquid.
2 Meanwhile, make remoulade.
3 Place yabbies, upside down, on board;
   cut tails from bodies, discard bodies. Cut
   through tails lengthways; remove meat
   from shells. Chop meat coarsely; combine
   in bowl with chives, rind and juice.
4 Discard both ends of bread stick; cut
   bread into 1cm slices. Spread remoulade
   onto one side of each slice; spoon yabby
   mixture onto remoulade on each slice.

REMOULADE Blend or process egg
yolks, vinegar, mustard and the water until
combined. With motor operating,
gradually add oil in thin, steady stream
until remoulade mixture is thick and creamy.
Transfer to small bowl; stir in capers and dill.

makes 24

TIP Refrigerate any remaining remoulade,
covered, for up to five days.

CRAB RICE PAPER ROLLS

PREPARATION TIME 35 MINUTES

You need to buy half a small chinese cabbage for this recipe.

½ cup (125ml) mirin
⅓ cup (80ml) soy sauce
2 teaspoons fish sauce
2 teaspoons sesame oil
⅓ cup (80ml) lime juice
1 tablespoon sugar
⅓ cup finely chopped fresh coriander
500g cooked crab meat
2 cups (160g) finely shredded
    chinese cabbage
½ cup coarsely chopped fresh mint
1 medium carrot (120g), cut into
    matchsticks
1½ cups (120g) bean sprouts
1 cup (50g) snow pea sprouts
1 fresh small red thai chilli,
    chopped finely
20 x 16cm-round rice paper sheets

1 Combine mirin, sauces, oil, juice, sugar and coriander in small jug. Pour half of the mirin mixture into medium bowl, add crab; toss crab gently to coat in mixture.
2 Combine cabbage, mint, carrot, sprouts and chilli in large bowl.
3 Place 1 sheet of rice paper in medium bowl of warm water until just softened; lift from water carefully, place on board covered with tea towel. Place about ¼ cup of the cabbage mixture in centre of rice paper, top with about 1 tablespoon of the crab mixture. Fold in two opposing sides; roll to enclose filling. Repeat with remaining rice paper sheets, cabbage mixture and crab mixture.
4 Serve rolls with remaining mirin mixture as a dipping sauce.

makes 20

TIP Lobster or prawn meat can be substituted for the crab, if desired.

OYSTERS

OYSTERS WITH LIME AND WASABI

PREPARATION TIME 5 MINUTES

2 tablespoons lime juice
1 teaspoon wasabi paste
1 tablespoon rice vinegar
2 teaspoons vegetable oil
2 teaspoons finely chopped fresh coriander
12 oysters, on the half shell

1 Place juice, wasabi, vinegar, oil and coriander in screw-top jar; shake well.
2 Divide mixture among oysters. Serve immediately.

makes 12

OYSTERS WITH RED WINE VINEGAR

PREPARATION TIME 5 MINUTES

¼ cup (60ml) red wine vinegar
1 shallot (25g), chopped finely
¼ teaspoon cracked black pepper
12 oysters, on the half shell

1 Place vinegar, shallot and pepper in screw-top jar; shake well.
2 Divide mixture among oysters. Serve immediately.

makes 12

OYSTERS WITH CHIVE BECHAMEL

PREPARATION TIME 5 MINUTES

COOKING TIME 15 MINUTES

20g butter
1 tablespoon plain flour
½ cup (125ml) milk
pinch dried chilli flakes
1 tablespoon finely chopped fresh chives
12 oysters, on the half shell

1 Preheat grill.
2 Melt butter in small saucepan; add flour, stir until mixture bubbles and thickens. Gradually add milk; stir until mixture boils and thickens. Remove from heat. Stir in chilli and chives.
3 Place oysters on oven tray; top with chive mixture. Place under preheated grill about 5 minutes or until browned lightly. Serve immediately.

makes 12

OYSTERS WITH SAUCE CUORE

PREPARATION TIME 10 MINUTES

COOKING TIME 10 MINUTES

1 tablespoon olive oil
½ small red onion (50g), chopped finely
1 clove garlic, crushed
2 slices prosciutto (30g), chopped finely
300g tomatoes, seeded, chopped finely
1 tablespoon finely shredded fresh basil
12 oysters, on the half shell
2 tablespoons finely grated parmesan cheese

1 Preheat grill.
2 Heat oil in small frying pan; cook onion and garlic, stirring, until softened. Add prosciutto and tomato; cook, stirring, until tomato softens. Stir in basil.
3 Place oysters on oven tray; top with tomato mixture, sprinkle with cheese. Place under preheated grill about 5 minutes or until cheese melts. Serve immediately.

makes 12

SLOW-COOKED SPICY HERBED PRAWNS

PREPARATION TIME 20 MINUTES **COOKING TIME** 30 MINUTES (PLUS REFRIGERATION TIME)

2kg uncooked medium
  king prawns
4 cloves garlic, crushed
2 fresh long red chillies,
  chopped coarsely
¾ cup (180ml) olive oil
½ cup (125ml) lemon juice
1 teaspoon sweet paprika
½ cup loosely packed fresh
  flat-leaf parsley leaves
½ cup loosely packed fresh
  coriander leaves
¼ cup coarsely chopped
  fresh chives

1 Preheat oven to slow.
2 Shell and devein prawns, leaving
   tails intact.
3 Combine garlic, chilli, oil, juice and
   paprika in shallow 3-litre (12-cup)
   baking dish, add prawns; toss
   prawns gently to coat in mixture.
   Cook, covered, in slow oven
   about 30 minutes or until prawns
   are just cooked through; stirring
   once halfway through cooking
   time. Cover; refrigerate 2 hours.
4 Serve prawns tossed with herbs.

serves 8

SMOKED SALMON AND DILLED SOUR CREAM CREPE CAKES

PREPARATION TIME 30 MINUTES (PLUS STANDING TIME) **COOKING TIME** 30 MINUTES (PLUS REFRIGERATION TIME)

½ cup (75g) plain flour

2 eggs

2 teaspoons vegetable oil

1 cup (250ml) milk

2 tablespoons drained capers,
 rinsed, chopped coarsely

2 tablespoons finely chopped
 fresh dill

1 tablespoon grated lemon rind

2 teaspoons lemon juice

1 clove garlic, crushed

1 cup (240g) sour cream

500g sliced smoked salmon

1 Line base and side of deep 20cm-round cake pan with plastic wrap.

2 Place flour in medium bowl. Make well in centre; gradually whisk in combined eggs, oil and milk. Strain into large jug; stand 30 minutes.

3 Heat oiled 19cm frying pan; pour ¼ cup of the batter into pan, tilting pan to coat base. Cook over low heat, loosening around edge with spatula until browned lightly. Turn; brown other side. Remove from pan; repeat with remaining batter to make a total of five crepes.

4 Combine capers, dill, rind, juice, garlic and sour cream in small bowl. Place a crepe in prepared pan; spread with ⅓ cup of sour cream mixture, cover with a quarter of the fish. Continue layering with remaining crepes, sour cream mixture and fish, finishing with a crepe. Cover; refrigerate overnight.

5 Gently turn cake onto chopping board; discard plastic wrap. Using sharp knife, carefully trim cake into a square; discard trimmings. Cut into 4cm squares; top squares with sour cream and dill, if desired.

makes 16

These four recipes will serve six as an antipasto platter.

ANTIPASTO

MARINATED BOCCONCINI

PREPARATION TIME 10 MINUTES
(PLUS REFRIGERATION TIME)

2 tablespoons olive oil
1 fresh long red chilli, chopped finely
1 tablespoon finely chopped fresh flat-leaf parsley
1 tablespoon finely grated lemon rind
12 bocconcini cheese (720g), halved
2 tablespoons lemon juice

1 Combine oil, chilli, parsley and rind in medium bowl, add cheese; toss cheese to coat in marinade. Cover; refrigerate 3 hours or overnight.
2 Drain cheese mixture before serving drizzled with juice and lemon wedges, if desired.

SPICY PRAWNS

PREPARATION TIME 15 MINUTES
(PLUS REFRIGERATION TIME)
COOKING TIME 10 MINUTES

18 uncooked medium king prawns (720g)
2 cloves garlic, crushed
1 fresh long red chilli, chopped finely
2 tablespoons olive oil
1 tablespoon lemon juice

1 Shell and devein prawns, leaving tails intact. Combine garlic, chilli and oil in medium bowl, add prawns; toss prawns to coat in marinade. Cover; refrigerate 3 hours or overnight.
2 Cook prawns in large heated frying pan, in batches, until just changed in colour. Serve prawns drizzled with juice.

PAN-FRIED ASPARAGUS WITH PARMESAN

PREPARATION TIME 5 MINUTES
COOKING TIME 5 MINUTES

1 tablespoon olive oil
400g asparagus, trimmed
½ cup (40g) flaked parmesan cheese
½ teaspoon cracked black pepper

1 Heat oil in large frying pan; cook asparagus, in batches, until just tender.
2 Serve asparagus sprinkled with cheese and cracked pepper.

PUMPKIN AND SPINACH FRITTATA

PREPARATION TIME 20 MINUTES
(PLUS REFRIGERATION TIME)
COOKING TIME 45 MINUTES

900g pumpkin, sliced thinly
2 cloves garlic, crushed
1 tablespoon olive oil
6 eggs
½ cup (125ml) cream
40g baby spinach leaves
¼ cup (20g) coarsely grated parmesan cheese

1 Preheat oven to moderately hot.
2 Place pumpkin, in single layer, on baking trays; brush with combined garlic and oil. Roast, uncovered, in moderately hot oven until tender.
3 Meanwhile, oil deep 20cm-square cake pan; line base and sides with baking paper.
4 Whisk eggs with cream in medium jug. Layer half of the pumpkin in prepared pan; pour half of the egg mixture over pumpkin. Top with spinach and remaining pumpkin then pour in remaining egg mixture; sprinkle with cheese.
5 Bake, uncovered, in moderately hot oven about 25 minutes or until firm. Stand 5 minutes before cutting into triangles.

ROASTED VEGETABLE AND GOAT CHEESE TERRINE

PREPARATION TIME 30 MINUTES **COOKING TIME** 25 MINUTES (PLUS REFRIGERATION TIME)

2 large red capsicums (700g)
2 large eggplants (1kg), sliced thinly lengthways
2 medium green zucchini (240g), sliced
  thinly lengthways
150g soft goat cheese
¼ cup (60ml) cream
1 tablespoon lemon juice
½ cup loosely packed fresh basil leaves
100g mixed salad leaves

BASIL OIL
½ cup (125ml) extra virgin olive oil
½ cup loosely packed fresh basil leaves
10g baby spinach leaves
1 tablespoon finely grated lemon rind

1 Line 1.5-litre (6-cup) terrine dish with plastic wrap.
2 Quarter capsicums; discard seeds and membranes. Roast under grill or in very hot oven, skin-side up, until skin blisters and blackens. Cover capsicum pieces in plastic or paper 5 minutes; peel away skin.
3 Cook eggplant and zucchini in lightly oiled large frying pan, in batches, until browned both sides.
4 Combine cheese, cream and juice in small bowl.
5 Line base and sides of prepared dish with two-thirds of the eggplant, draping eggplant over all sides of dish. Place half of the capsicum over base of dish; spread cheese mixture over capsicum then top with basil, zucchini, remaining capsicum and remaining eggplant. Fold overhanging eggplant at short sides over terrine then fold remaining eggplant over long sides to completely enclose terrine. Cover; refrigerate 30 minutes.
6 Meanwhile, make basil oil.
7 Cut terrine into eight slices. Serve on salad leaves, drizzle with basil oil.

BASIL OIL Blend or process ingredients until smooth. Strain through small muslin-lined strainer into small jug.

serves 8

COCONUT CHICKEN SALAD IN CRISP WONTON CUPS

PREPARATION TIME 25 MINUTES **COOKING TIME** 25 MINUTES (PLUS COOLING TIME)

You need four 12-hole mini muffin pans for this recipe. If you don't own four, make the wonton cups in batches, cooling one batch on a wire rack while you bake another.

350g chicken breast fillets
¾ cup (180ml) chicken stock
1 cup (250ml) coconut cream
4 fresh kaffir lime leaves, shredded finely
1 tablespoon brown sugar
1 tablespoon fish sauce
1 clove garlic, crushed
1 fresh small red thai chilli, chopped finely
40 square wonton wrappers
cooking-oil spray
100g snow peas, trimmed, sliced thinly
½ cup finely chopped fresh coriander

1   Preheat oven to moderately hot. Lightly oil four 12-hole mini (1-tablespoon/20ml) muffin pans.
2   Combine chicken, stock, coconut cream and lime leaves in medium saucepan; bring to a boil. Reduce heat; simmer, uncovered, about 10 minutes or until chicken is cooked through. Cool chicken in coconut mixture 10 minutes.
3   Remove chicken from coconut mixture; chop chicken finely. Bring coconut mixture to a boil. Reduce heat; simmer, uncovered, until mixture reduces by half. Strain into medium bowl; stir sugar, fish sauce, garlic and chilli into dressing. Cool to room temperature.
4   Meanwhile, push wonton wrappers into holes of prepared pans; spray lightly with oil. Bake, uncovered, in moderately hot oven about 7 minutes or until wonton cups are browned lightly. Stand in pans 2 minutes; turn onto wire racks to cool.
5   Stir chicken, snow peas and coriander into dressing in bowl; divide chicken mixture among wonton cups.

makes 40

TRADITIONAL TURKEY WITH FORCEMEAT STUFFING

PREPARATION TIME 40 MINUTES

COOKING TIME 3 HOURS 10 MINUTES (PLUS STANDING TIME)

We've used pork and chicken in our forcemeat stuffing, however, you can use your favourite mixture of fish, poultry, meat, vegetables or fruit with breadcrumbs and various seasonings. This recipe will serve between eight and 12 people depending on your menu.

4.5kg turkey

1 cup (250ml) water

80g butter, melted

¼ cup (35g) plain flour

3 cups (750ml) chicken stock

½ cup (125ml) dry white wine

FORCEMEAT STUFFING

40g butter

3 medium brown onions (450g), chopped finely

2 bacon rashers (140g), rind removed, chopped coarsely

1 cup (70g) stale breadcrumbs

2 tablespoons finely chopped fresh tarragon

½ cup coarsely chopped fresh flat-leaf parsley

½ cup (75g) coarsely chopped roasted pistachios

250g pork mince

250g chicken mince

1 Make forcemeat stuffing.

2 Preheat oven to moderate.

3 Discard neck from turkey. Rinse turkey under cold water; pat dry inside and out with absorbent paper. Fill neck cavity loosely with stuffing; secure skin over opening with toothpicks. Fill large cavity loosely with stuffing; tie legs together with kitchen string.

4 Place turkey on oiled wire rack in large shallow flameproof baking dish; pour the water into dish. Brush turkey all over with half of the butter; cover dish tightly with two layers of greased foil. Roast in moderate oven 2 hours. Uncover turkey; brush with remaining butter. Roast, uncovered, in moderate oven about 45 minutes or until browned all over and cooked through. Remove turkey from dish, cover turkey; stand 20 minutes.

5 Pour juice from dish into large jug; skim 1 tablespoon of the fat from juice, return to same dish. Skim and discard remaining fat from juice. Add flour to dish; cook, stirring, until mixture bubbles and is well browned. Gradually stir in stock, wine and remaining juice; bring to a boil, stirring, until gravy boils and thickens. Strain gravy into same jug; serve turkey with gravy.

FORCEMEAT STUFFING Melt butter in medium frying pan; cook onion and bacon, stirring, until onion softens. Using hand, combine onion mixture in large bowl with remaining ingredients.

TIP To test if turkey is cooked, insert a skewer sideways into the thickest part of the thigh then remove and press flesh to release the juices. If the juice runs clear, the turkey is cooked. Alternatively, insert a meat thermometer into the thickest part of the thigh, without touching bone; it should reach 90°C.

POMEGRANATE-GLAZED TURKEY WITH CORNBREAD SEASONING

PREPARATION TIME I HOUR 30 MINUTES

COOKING TIME 3 HOURS 30 MINUTES (PLUS COOLING AND STANDING TIME)

1 Two days before, make macerated fruit.
2 On the day you want to roast the turkey, preheat oven to moderate.
3 Discard neck from turkey. Rinse turkey under cold water; pat dry inside and out with absorbent paper.
4 Heat butter in large saucepan; cook whole shallots and apple, stirring, until browned lightly. Cool 10 minutes; stir in sage and peppercorns. Tuck wings under turkey; fill large cavity loosely with stuffing; tie legs together with kitchen string.
5 Place turkey on oiled wire rack in large shallow flameproof baking dish; pour the water, stock and brandy into dish. Brush turkey all over with melted butter; cover dish tightly with two layers of greased foil. Roast in moderate oven 2 hours 10 minutes.
6 Meanwhile, make cornbread seasoning.
7 Uncover turkey; brush with half of the molasses. Roast, uncovered, in moderate oven about 20 minutes or until browned all over and cooked through, brushing frequently with remaining molasses. Remove turkey from dish, cover turkey; stand 20 minutes.
8 Pour juice from dish into large jug; skim 1 tablespoon of the fat from juice, return to same dish. Skim and discard remaining fat from juice. Add flour to dish; cook, stirring, until mixture bubbles and is well browned. Gradually stir in juice; bring to a boil, stirring, until gravy boils and thickens. Strain gravy into same jug; serve turkey with cornbread seasoning and gravy.

MACERATED FRUIT Combine ingredients in small glass jar, cover; stand at room temperature for two days.

CORNBREAD SEASONING Line 7cm x 21cm loaf pan with baking paper, extending paper 5cm over long sides. Cook chorizo in large frying pan, stirring, until browned lightly. Add onion and shallot; cook, stirring, until onion softens. Add apple; cook, stirring, until browned lightly. Remove from heat; stir in sage, juice, cornbread and macerated fruit. Place seasoning in prepared pan in oven alongside turkey; cook, uncovered, in moderate oven during last 30 minutes of turkey roasting time.

TIP To test if turkey is cooked, insert a skewer sideways into the thickest part of the thigh then remove and press flesh to release the juices. If the juice runs clear, the turkey is cooked. Alternatively, insert a meat thermometer into the thickest part of the thigh, without touching bone; it should reach 90°C.

This recipe will serve between eight and 12 people depending on your menu. The cornbread seasoning can be made a day ahead.

4kg turkey
20g butter
6 shallots (150g)
1 large apple (200g), cut into 6 wedges
1 tablespoon fresh sage leaves
20 black peppercorns
2 cups (500ml) water
1 cup (250ml) chicken stock
½ cup (125ml) brandy
50g butter, melted
½ cup (125ml) pomegranate molasses
2 tablespoons plain flour

MACERATED FRUIT

¼ cup (35g) coarsely chopped dried apricots
¼ cup (35g) dried currants
⅓ cup (80ml) brandy

CORNBREAD SEASONING

350g chorizo, chopped finely
1 medium brown onion (150g), chopped coarsely
2 shallots (50g), chopped coarsely
1 large apple (200g), chopped coarsely
1 tablespoon fresh sage leaves, torn
2 cups (500ml) apple juice
3½ cups (340g) coarsely chopped stale cornbread
⅔ cup (180g) macerated fruit

BONED TURKEY BUFFE WITH COUSCOUS STUFFING

PREPARATION TIME 1 HOUR
COOKING TIME 2 HOURS

Order a 4.5kg fresh boned and butterflied turkey buffé from your butcher for this recipe.
This recipe will serve between eight and 12 people depending on your menu.

½ cup (80g) sultanas
½ cup (125ml) lemon juice
4.5kg butterflied turkey buffé
1 cup (250ml) chicken stock
¼ cup (60ml) olive oil
1 cup (200g) couscous
¼ cup (40g) toasted pepitas
¼ cup (35g) toasted slivered almonds
¼ cup (35g) toasted pecans, chopped coarsely
¼ cup coarsely chopped fresh flat-leaf parsley
¼ cup coarsely chopped fresh coriander
2 eggs, beaten lightly
1 cup (250ml) water
½ cup (125ml) dry white wine
⅓ cup (50g) plain flour
2 cups (500ml) chicken stock, extra
3 cups (750ml) water, extra

PAPRIKA RUB

1 teaspoon fennel seeds
1 teaspoon sweet paprika
½ teaspoon ground ginger
2 teaspoons salt
2 cloves garlic, quartered
2 tablespoons olive oil

1 Soak sultanas in small bowl in half of the juice. Make paprika rub.

2 Preheat oven to moderate.

3 Place turkey flat on board, skin-side down; cover with plastic wrap. Using rolling pin or meat mallet, flatten turkey meat to an even thickness all over.

4 Combine stock, oil and remaining juice in medium saucepan; bring to a boil. Remove from heat; stir in couscous. Cover; stand about 5 minutes or until liquid is absorbed, fluffing with fork occasionally. Transfer couscous mixture to large bowl; stir in sultana mixture, pepitas, nuts, herbs and egg.

5 With pointed end of turkey breast facing away from you, place couscous stuffing horizontally along centre of turkey meat. Bring the pointed end of breast over stuffing, securing to the neck skin flap with toothpicks. Working from the centre out, continue securing sides of turkey together with toothpicks (you will have a rectangular roll of turkey in front of you). Tie securely with kitchen string at 4cm intervals.

6 Place turkey roll on oiled wire rack in large shallow flameproof baking dish; add the water and wine to dish. Rub turkey roll with paprika rub; cover dish tightly with two layers of greased foil. Roast in moderate oven 1 hour. Uncover; roast in moderate oven about 45 minutes or until turkey roll is cooked though. Transfer turkey roll to large serving platter; cover to keep warm.

7 Place dish with juice over heat, add flour; cook, stirring, until mixture bubbles and is well browned. Gradually stir in the extra stock and the extra water; bring to a boil. Reduce heat; simmer, stirring, until gravy boils and thickens. Strain gravy into large jug; serve with turkey.

PAPRIKA RUB Using mortar and pestle, crush ingredients until smooth.

ASIAN-SPICED BARBECUED TURKEY

PREPARATION TIME 25 MINUTES **COOKING TIME** 1 HOUR 50 MINUTES

1 Discard neck from turkey. Rinse turkey under cold water; pat dry inside and out with absorbent paper. Using kitchen scissors, cut along each side of turkey's backbone; discard backbone. Turn turkey skin-side up; using heel of hand, press down on breastbone to flatten turkey.

2 Using mortar and pestle, crush peppercorns, star anise, seeds and salt until mixture is crushed coarsely. Dry-fry peppercorn mixture with chilli, ginger and five-spice, in small frying pan, until fragrant. Remove from heat; stir in oil. Rub all over turkey.

3 Place turkey on heated barbecue; cook, covered, using indirect method, over low heat about 1¾ hours or until cooked through.

4 Meanwhile, make peach and craisin chutney.

5 Serve turkey with chutney.

PEACH AND CRAISIN CHUTNEY Place peaches in large bowl, cover with boiling water for 30 seconds; drain, peel, seed. Chop peaches coarsely, combine in medium saucepan with remaining ingredients; bring to a boil. Reduce heat; simmer, uncovered, stirring occasionally, about 1¼ hours or until chutney thickens.

TIP Chutney can be made up to three months ahead and stored in sterilised jars.

This recipe will serve between eight and 12 people depending on your menu. You can ask your butcher to butterfly the turkey for you if you wish.

4kg turkey
2 tablespoons sichuan peppercorns
2 star anise
1 tablespoon coriander seeds
1 tablespoon cumin seeds
2 teaspoons salt
2 teaspoons dried chilli flakes
1 teaspoon ground ginger
1 teaspoon five-spice powder
⅓ cup (80ml) olive oil

PEACH AND CRAISIN CHUTNEY

7 large peaches (1.5kg)
1 cup (250ml) cider vinegar
¼ cup (60ml) lemon juice
1 cup (150g) craisins
1 small brown onion (80g), chopped finely
½ teaspoon ground cinnamon
½ teaspoon ground cloves
½ teaspoon ground ginger
½ teaspoon ground allspice
2 cups (440g) caster sugar

Using kitchen scissors, cut along both sides of backbone then discard bone.

Press down on breastbone with the heel of your hand to flatten turkey.

Rub peppercorn-spice mixture all over turkey, inside and out, with your hands.

31

ASIAN-STYLE BAKED HAM

PREPARATION TIME 15 MINUTES (PLUS REFRIGERATION TIME)
COOKING TIME 1 HOUR 30 MINUTES

This recipe will serve between eight and 12 people depending on your menu.

7kg cooked leg of ham
1 cup (250ml) soy sauce
¾ cup (180ml) dry sherry
⅓ cup (75g) firmly packed brown sugar
⅓ cup (120g) honey
2 teaspoons red food colouring
4 cloves garlic, crushed
2 teaspoons five-spice powder
60 cloves (approximately)

1 Cut through rind about 10cm from shank end of leg in decorative pattern; run thumb around edge of rind just under skin to remove rind. Start pulling rind from shank end to widest edge of ham; discard rind.

2 Using sharp knife, make shallow cuts in one direction diagonally across fat at 3cm intervals, then shallow-cut in opposite direction, forming diamonds. Do not cut through top fat or fat will spread apart during cooking.

3 Combine soy, sherry, sugar, honey, colouring, garlic and five-spice in small bowl. Place ham on wire rack in large baking dish; brush ham with soy mixture. Centre a clove in each diamond shape, cover; refrigerate overnight.

4 Preheat oven to moderate.

5 Place ham on wire rack in large baking dish; pour marinade into small jug. Cover ham with greased foil; bake in moderate oven 1 hour. Uncover; bake in moderate oven about 30 minutes or until ham is lightly caramelised, brushing frequently with marinade during cooking.

TIP As an alternative to the Asian flavours used above, a glaze of orange, ginger and maple syrup also goes beautifully with this ham. Combine 1 cup maple syrup, 1 cup fresh orange juice, ⅓ cup orange marmalade, ¼ cup grated fresh ginger and 2 teaspoons finely grated orange rind in small saucepan; bring to a boil. Reduce heat; simmer, uncovered, 15 minutes then strain before brushing over ham during baking.

AUSSIE BARBECUED HAM

PREPARATION TIME 15 MINUTES

COOKING TIME 1 HOUR 45 MINUTES (PLUS STANDING TIME)

1 Cut through rind about 10cm from shank end of leg in decorative pattern; run thumb around edge of rind just under skin to remove rind. Start pulling rind from shank end to widest edge of ham; discard rind.

2 Using sharp knife, make shallow cuts in one direction diagonally across fat at 3cm intervals, then shallow-cut in opposite direction, forming diamonds. Do not cut through top fat or fat will spread apart during cooking.

3 Place ham in disposable aluminium baking dish; rub with combined mustard and sugar. Place ham on heated barbecue; cook, covered, using indirect method, 1 hour.

4 Meanwhile, combine juice, sherry, extra sugar, garlic and clove in small saucepan; stir over heat until sugar dissolves. Reduce heat; simmer, uncovered, about 10 minutes or until glaze reduces by half. Brush ham with glaze; cook, covered, using indirect method, 45 minutes, brushing several times with glaze during cooking. Cover ham with foil; stand 15 minutes before slicing.

5 Meanwhile, cook pineapple on heated barbecue, brushing with remaining glaze during cooking.

6 Serve ham with pineapple.

TIP As an alternative to the Aussie flavours used above, a glaze of redcurrant cranberry sauce and port also goes beautifully with this ham. Combine a 275g jar red currant and cranberry sauce and ½ cup (125ml) water in small saucepan; stir over heat, without boiling, until sauce is smooth. Remove from heat, stir in 2 tablespoons lemon juice and ⅓ cup (80ml) port; brush over ham during last 45 minutes of cooking time.

This recipe will serve between eight and 12 people depending on your menu.

7kg cooked leg of ham
2 tablespoons dijon mustard
⅔ cup (150g) firmly packed
   brown sugar
½ cup (125ml) pineapple juice
½ cup (125ml) sweet sherry
¼ cup (55g) firmly packed
   brown sugar, extra
2 cloves garlic, halved lengthways
¼ teaspoon ground clove
1 medium pineapple (1.25kg), halved,
   sliced thickly

PORK LOIN WITH SPINACH AND PANCETTA STUFFING

PREPARATION TIME 30 MINUTES

COOKING TIME 1 HOUR 30 MINUTES

When you order the pork loin, ask your butcher to leave a flap measuring about 20cm in length to help make rolling the stuffed loin easier. This recipe will serve between eight and 12 people depending on your menu.

4 slices white bread (120g)

2 tablespoons olive oil

1 clove garlic, crushed

1 medium brown onion (150g), chopped coarsely

6 slices pancetta (90g), chopped coarsely

100g baby spinach leaves

¼ cup (35g) toasted macadamias, chopped coarsely

½ cup (125ml) chicken stock

2kg boned pork loin

PLUM AND RED WINE SAUCE

1½ cups (480g) plum jam

2 tablespoons dry red wine

⅔ cup (160ml) chicken stock

1 Preheat oven to moderately hot.

2 Discard bread crusts; cut bread into 1cm cubes. Heat half of the oil in large frying pan; cook bread, stirring, until browned and crisp. Drain croutons on absorbent paper.

3 Heat remaining oil in same pan; cook garlic, onion and pancetta until onion browns lightly. Stir in spinach; remove from heat. Gently stir in croutons, nuts and stock.

4 Place pork on board, fat-side down; slice through thickest part of pork horizontally, without cutting through other side. Open out pork to form one large piece; press stuffing mixture against loin along width of pork. Roll pork to enclose stuffing, securing with kitchen string at 2cm intervals.

5 Place rolled pork on rack in large shallow baking dish. Roast, uncovered, in moderately hot oven about 1¼ hours or until cooked through.

6 Meanwhile, make plum and red wine sauce.

7 Serve sliced pork with sauce.

PLUM AND RED WINE SAUCE Combine ingredients in small saucepan; bring to a boil. Reduce heat; simmer, uncovered, about 10 minutes or until sauce thickens slightly.

Slice through the thickest part of the pork, without cutting through the other side.

Press stuffing mixture against the loin across the entire width of the pork.

Roll pork to enclose stuffing; secure loin with kitchen string at 2cm intervals.

CARAMELISED BARBECUED PORK NECK

PREPARATION TIME 15 MINUTES

COOKING TIME 1 HOUR 30 MINUTES (PLUS STANDING TIME)

1 Make hot and sweet glaze.

2 Using sharp knife, make eight small cuts in pork. Press garlic, ginger and star anise pieces into cuts; rub pork with salt. Brush ¼ cup of the glaze over pork.

3 Place pork on heated barbecue; cook, covered, over low heat 30 minutes. Turn pork; cook, covered, further 30 minutes. Uncover; cook pork 10 minutes, brushing with remaining glaze constantly. Increase heat to high; cook 5 minutes, turning and brushing with glaze constantly. Remove pork from heat; stand 15 minutes before slicing.

HOT AND SWEET GLAZE Combine the water and sugar in medium saucepan; bring to a boil. Reduce heat; simmer, uncovered, about 10 minutes or until glaze thickens slightly. Remove from heat; stir in chillies, star anise, soy and juice.

serves 8

1.2kg piece pork neck

1 clove garlic, sliced thinly

4cm piece fresh ginger (20g), sliced thinly

2 star anise, quartered

2 tablespoons sea salt

HOT AND SWEET GLAZE

1¼ cups (310ml) water

1¾ cups (400g) grated palm sugar

3 fresh long red chillies, sliced thinly

2 fresh small red thai chillies, sliced thinly

1 star anise

⅓ cup (80ml) soy sauce

½ cup (125ml) lime juice

HERBED BEEF FILLET WITH HORSERADISH CREAM SAUCE

PREPARATION TIME 15 MINUTES

COOKING TIME 40 MINUTES

1 tablespoon finely grated lemon rind

⅓ cup (80ml) lemon juice

1 teaspoon dried chilli flakes

3 cloves garlic, crushed

¼ cup coarsely chopped fresh
flat-leaf parsley

¼ cup loosely packed fresh
oregano leaves

¼ cup coarsely chopped fresh basil

¼ cup loosely packed fresh
marjoram leaves

⅓ cup (80ml) olive oil

2kg piece beef tenderloin

HORSERADISH CREAM SAUCE

1 tablespoon olive oil

2 cloves garlic, crushed

2 teaspoons plain flour

½ cup (125ml) dry white wine

½ cup (140g) horseradish cream

600ml cream

1 Preheat oven to moderately hot.

2 Combine rind, juice, chilli, garlic, herbs and oil in large bowl, add beef; roll beef to coat in herb mixture. Place beef on oiled wire rack in large shallow baking dish. Roast, uncovered, in moderately hot oven about 40 minutes or until cooked as desired. Cover beef; stand 10 minutes.

3 Meanwhile, make horseradish cream sauce.

4 Serve sliced beef with sauce.

HORSERADISH CREAM SAUCE Heat oil in small frying pan; cook garlic and flour, stirring, until mixtures bubbles and browns lightly. Gradually stir in wine; bring to a boil, stirring. Reduce heat; simmer, uncovered, until liquid reduces by half. Stir in horseradish and cream; simmer, stirring, about 5 minutes or until sauce thickens slightly.

serves 8

CHAR-GRILLED POULTRY PLATTER

PREPARATION TIME 20 MINUTES (PLUS REFRIGERATION TIME)
COOKING TIME 30 MINUTES

1 Make lemon dressing.

2 Combine duck in medium bowl with ¼ cup of the dressing and half of the chilli; toss duck to coat in chilli marinade. Combine chicken, spatchcock and quail in large bowl with remaining dressing; toss to coat in lemon marinade. Cover each bowl; refrigerate 3 hours or overnight.

3 Drain duck over small bowl; reserve chilli marinade. Drain chicken, spatchcock and quail over medium bowl; reserve lemon marinade. Cook chicken, spatchcock and quail, in batches, on heated oiled grill plate (or grill or barbecue) until cooked through. During cooking, brush chicken with reserved lemon marinade, spatchcock with ¼ cup of the kecap manis, and quail with honey. Brush duck with reserved chilli marinade; cook as desired.

4 Cook tomatoes on same heated oiled grill plate about 5 minutes or until just softened.

5 Cut duck into thick slices. Place spinach on large serving platter; arrange poultry and tomatoes on platter. Sprinkle duck with remaining chilli; drizzle spatchcock with remaining kecap manis.

LEMON DRESSING Dry-fry cumin and coriander in small heated frying pan, stirring, until fragrant. Combine spice mixture in small jug with oil and juice.

serves 8

4 duck breast fillets (800g), trimmed
2 fresh long red chillies, sliced thinly
8 chicken drumsticks (1.2kg)
2 x 500g spatchcocks, quartered
4 quails (800g), halved
⅓ cup (80ml) kecap manis
¼ cup (90g) honey
300g baby vine-ripened truss tomatoes
100g baby spinach leaves

LEMON DRESSING

1 teaspoon ground cumin
2 teaspoons ground coriander
½ cup (125ml) olive oil
¾ cup (180ml) lemon juice

SALT-CRUSTED OCEAN TROUT WITH THAI-FLAVOURS HOLLANDAISE

PREPARATION TIME 20 MINUTES **COOKING TIME** I HOUR I5 MINUTES

Cooking salt is coarser than table salt, but not as large-flaked as sea salt: it is sold packaged in bags in most supermarkets. You'll need a very large (approximately 30cm x 40cm) baking dish in order to fit in the whole fish.

2kg cooking salt
3 egg whites
2.4kg whole ocean trout

THAI-FLAVOURS HOLLANDAISE

10cm stick (20g) fresh lemon grass
2 tablespoons water
½ cup (125ml) white wine vinegar
1 tablespoon lemon juice
1 teaspoon black peppercorns
1 tablespoon finely chopped fresh
   lemon grass
6 egg yolks
250g butter, melted
2 tablespoons lime juice
4 fresh kaffir lime leaves,
   shredded finely

1 Preheat oven to moderately hot.

2 Combine salt with egg whites in medium bowl (mixture will resemble wet sand). Spread about half of the salt mixture evenly over base of shallow 30cm x 40cm baking dish; place fish on salt mixture then cover completely (except for tail) with remaining salt mixture. Cook fish in moderately hot oven 1 hour.

3 Meanwhile, make thai-flavours hollandaise.

4 Remove fish from oven; break salt crust with heavy knife, taking care not to cut into fish. Discard salt crust; transfer fish to large serving platter.

5 Carefully remove skin from fish; flake fish into large pieces. Serve fish with hollandaise.

THAI-FLAVOURS HOLLANDAISE Bruise lemon grass stick with side of heavy knife. Combine lemon grass stick with the water, vinegar, juice and peppercorns in small saucepan; bring to a boil. Reduce heat; simmer, uncovered, until mixture reduces to 2 tablespoons. Discard lemon grass stick; stir in chopped lemon grass; cool 10 minutes. Combine vinegar mixture with egg yolks in medium heatproof bowl over medium saucepan of simmering water; whisk mixture constantly about 5 minutes or until thickened. Gradually add butter in thin, steady stream, whisking constantly until mixture thickens. Whisk in juice and lime leaves.

serves 8

Stir the salt with egg whites in medium bowl until mixture resembles wet sand.

Sit fish on salt mixture in dish then cover all but the tail with remaining mixture.

Using the side of a large heavy knife, press firmly on the lemon grass stalk to bruise it.

SLOW-ROASTED PESTO SALMON

PREPARATION TIME 20 MINUTES
COOKING TIME 45 MINUTES

1 Preheat oven to moderately slow.

2 Blend or process basil, garlic, nuts and juice until combined. With motor operating, gradually add oil in thin, steady stream until pesto thickens slightly.

3 Place fish, skin-side down, on piece of lightly oiled foil large enough to completely enclose fish; coat fish with half of the pesto. Gather corners of foil together above fish; twist to enclose securely. Place parcel on oven tray; roast in moderately slow oven about 45 minutes or until cooked as desired.

4 Meanwhile, heat extra oil in large frying pan; cook capsicum and onion, stirring, until onion softens.

5 Place fish parcel on serving platter, unwrap; top with onion mixture, drizzle with remaining pesto.

serves 8

TIP If the pesto is a little too thick for your liking, thin it down with a little olive oil before drizzling over the salmon.

1 cup loosely packed fresh basil leaves

2 cloves garlic, chopped coarsely

2 tablespoons toasted pine nuts

2 tablespoons lemon juice

¼ cup (60ml) olive oil

1.5kg piece salmon fillet, skin on

2 tablespoons olive oil, extra

2 large red capsicums (700g), chopped coarsely

1 large red onion (300g), chopped coarsely

COLD SEAFOOD PLATTER

PREPARATION TIME 1 HOUR
COOKING TIME 35 MINUTES (PLUS COOLING TIME)

We have chosen to serve the prawns and octopus cold, but they also can be served hot, if you prefer, or even separately, with a green salad, for a light lunch or supper.

1kg uncooked medium king prawns
2 teaspoons dried chilli flakes
2 cloves garlic, crushed
1 medium orange (240g)
1 medium lemon (140g)
2 tablespoons olive oil
½ cup (125ml) water
2 bay leaves
700g cleaned baby octopus, quartered
2 cooked lobsters (2.4kg)
8 cooked balmain bugs (1.6kg)
24 oysters, on the half shell
⅔ cup (200g) whole-egg mayonnaise
1 tablespoon lemon juice, extra

HARISSA DIP

⅓ cup (50g) drained semi-dried
   tomatoes
1 tablespoon harissa paste
2 tablespoons lemon juice
¼ cup (60ml) olive oil
¼ cup (60ml) water

SALSA VERDE

½ cup firmly packed fresh flat-leaf
   parsley leaves
½ cup firmly packed fresh mint leaves
1 tablespoon drained capers, rinsed
2 drained anchovy fillets
¼ cup (60ml) olive oil
1 tablespoon lemon juice

1 Preheat oven to moderate.

2 Combine prawns, chilli and garlic in large baking dish; cover tightly with foil. Bake, uncovered, in moderate oven about 30 minutes or until prawns are changed in colour. Cool 1 hour.

3 Meanwhile, peel orange and lemon; combine rind in another large baking dish with peeled orange and lemon juices, oil, the water and bay leaves. Add octopus; toss gently to coat octopus in citrus mixture. Cover dish with foil; bake in moderate oven about 30 minutes or until tender. Cool 1 hour.

4 Meanwhile, make harissa dip and salsa verde.

5 Place one lobster upside-down, cut through chest and tail; turn lobster around and cut through head. Pull halves apart; using small spoon, remove brain matter and liver. Rinse lobster carefully under cold water; repeat with remaining lobster.

6 Turn one bug upside-down; cut off head. Using sharp knife, cut bug tail in half lengthways; carefully lift out and discard centre vein from tail. Repeat with remaining bugs.

7 Arrange lobster, bugs, prawn mixture and octopus mixture on large platter. Divide half of the salsa verde among oysters; arrange on same platter. Stir mayonnaise and extra juice into remaining salsa verde in small bowl; serve seafood platter with salsa verde mayonnaise and harissa dip.

HARISSA DIP Blend or process ingredients until smooth. Transfer to small bowl, cover; refrigerate until required.
SALSA VERDE Blend or process ingredients until just combined, cover; refrigerate until required.

serves 8

CORIANDER AND CHILLI-MARINATED SEAFOOD SALAD

PREPARATION TIME 35 MINUTES (PLUS REFRIGERATION TIME)
COOKING TIME 20 MINUTES

1 Make coriander and chilli marinade.
2 Shell and devein prawns, leaving tails intact. Place prawns in large bowl with octopus, salmon, squid, scallops and marinade; toss gently to combine. Cover; refrigerate 3 hours or overnight.
3 Cook marinated seafood, in batches, on heated oiled grill plate (or grill or barbecue) until browned all over and cooked as desired. Flake salmon into large pieces.
4 Meanwhile, scrub mussels; remove beards. Cook mussels, covered, on same heated oiled grill plate until mussels open (discard any that do not).
5 Make lime dressing.
6 Place seafood in large bowl with rocket, tomato, avocado, coriander and dressing; toss gently to combine.

CORIANDER AND CHILLI MARINADE Blend or process ingredients until combined.
LIME DRESSING Place ingredients in screw-top jar; shake well.

serves 8

1kg uncooked large king prawns
600g cleaned baby octopus, halved lengthways
400g piece salmon fillet, skin on
400g squid hoods, cleaned, cut into rings
16 scallops (400g), roe removed
16 small black mussels (400g)
200g rocket
250g cherry tomatoes, halved
2 large avocados (640g), sliced thickly
1 cup loosely packed fresh coriander leaves

CORIANDER AND CHILLI MARINADE

4 coriander roots
¼ cup loosely packed fresh coriander leaves
2 cloves garlic, crushed
1 small red onion (100g), chopped coarsely
2 fresh small red thai chillies, chopped coarsely
3 fresh long red chillies, chopped coarsely
¼ cup (60ml) red wine vinegar
½ cup (125ml) olive oil
⅓ cup (80ml) lime juice
1 teaspoon sugar

LIME DRESSING

2 tablespoons lime juice
¼ cup (60ml) peanut oil

MIDDLE-EASTERN ROASTED PUMPKIN, CARROT AND PARSNIP

PREPARATION TIME 20 MINUTES

COOKING TIME 25 MINUTES

900g piece pumpkin,
   unpeeled, sliced thinly
1 tablespoon olive oil
4 large carrots (720g),
   halved, sliced thickly
2 large parsnips (700g),
   chopped coarsely
⅓ cup firmly packed fresh
   flat-leaf parsley leaves
¼ cup (40g) toasted pine nuts

SPICE PASTE

2 cloves garlic, quartered
1 teaspoon cumin seeds
1 teaspoon coriander seeds
½ teaspoon ground cinnamon
1 teaspoon sea salt
1 tablespoon olive oil
20g butter
¼ cup (55g) firmly packed brown sugar
1½ cups (375ml) apple juice

1 Preheat oven to moderately hot.
2 Place pumpkin and oil in large baking dish; toss pumpkin to coat in oil. Roast, uncovered, in moderately hot oven about 25 minutes or until just tender.
3 Meanwhile, boil, steam or microwave carrot and parsnip, separately, until just tender; drain. Make spice paste.
4 Place vegetables, parsley and nuts in large bowl with spice mixture; toss gently to combine.

SPICE PASTE Using mortar and pestle or small electric spice blender, crush garlic, cumin, coriander, cinnamon, salt and oil until mixture forms a thick paste. Melt butter in large frying pan; cook paste, stirring, about 3 minutes or until fragrant. Add sugar and juice; bring to a boil. Cook, stirring, about 10 minutes or until spice mixture thickens slightly.

serves 8

PERFECT ROAST POTATOES

PREPARATION TIME 15 MINUTES

COOKING TIME 55 MINUTES

12 medium pontiac potatoes (2.5kg),
   halved lengthways
⅓ cup (80ml) olive oil

1 Preheat oven to hot. Oil oven tray.
2 Boil, steam or microwave potato 5 minutes; drain.
   Pat dry with absorbent paper; cool 10 minutes.
3 Rake rounded sides of potato gently with tines of
   fork; place potato, cut-side down, in single layer,
   on prepared tray. Brush with oil; roast, uncovered,
   in hot oven about 50 minutes or until potato is
   browned lightly and crisp.

serves 8

MEDITERRANEAN POTATO MASH

PREPARATION TIME 25 MINUTES

COOKING TIME 20 MINUTES

2.5kg sebago potatoes, chopped coarsely
100g butter, softened
1½ cups (375ml) hot milk
½ cup (75g) drained sun-dried tomatoes,
   chopped coarsely
¼ cup coarsely chopped fresh flat-leaf parsley

BALSAMIC DRESSING
¼ cup (60ml) balsamic vinegar
2 tablespoons olive oil

1 Boil, steam or microwave potato until tender; drain.
2 Meanwhile, make balsamic dressing.
3 Mash potato in large bowl with butter and milk until
   smooth. Stir in tomato and parsley.
4 Serve mash drizzled with dressing.

BALSAMIC DRESSING Place ingredients in
screw-top jar; shake well.

serves 8

BARBECUED KIPFLERS

PREPARATION TIME 10 MINUTES
COOKING TIME 30 MINUTES

12 kipfler potatoes (1.5kg), unpeeled
2 tablespoons fresh oregano leaves
¼ cup loosely packed fresh thyme leaves
1 tablespoon coarsely grated lemon rind
2 cloves garlic, crushed
⅓ cup (80ml) olive oil
¼ cup (60ml) lemon juice

1 Boil, steam or microwave potatoes until tender;
  drain. Halve potatoes lengthways.
2 Combine herbs, rind, garlic and oil in large bowl,
  add potato; toss potato to coat in mixture. Cook
  potato on heated oiled grill plate (or grill or barbecue)
  about 15 minutes or until browned and tender.
3 Serve potato drizzled with juice.

serves 8

MUSTARD AND HONEY-GLAZED ROASTED KUMARA

PREPARATION TIME 10 MINUTES
COOKING TIME 1 HOUR

2.5kg kumara, unpeeled
⅔ cup (240g) honey
⅓ cup (95g) wholegrain mustard
2 tablespoons coarsely chopped fresh rosemary

1 Preheat oven to hot.
2 Halve kumara lengthways; cut each half into
  2cm wedges.
3 Combine remaining ingredients in large bowl,
  add kumara; toss kumara to coat in mixture.
  Divide kumara mixture between two large
  shallow baking dishes. Roast, uncovered, in
  hot oven about 1 hour or until kumara is tender
  and slightly caramelised.

serves 8

GREEN SALAD WITH ORANGE VINAIGRETTE

PREPARATION TIME 20 MINUTES **COOKING TIME** 20 MINUTES

150g sugar snap peas, trimmed

150g snow peas, trimmed

100g mizuna leaves

1 cup firmly packed fresh
   coriander leaves

1 cup firmly packed fresh
   flat-leaf parsley leaves

1 cup firmly packed fresh
   mint leaves

1 cup firmly packed fresh
   chervil sprigs

1 green oak leaf lettuce,
   trimmed, torn

ORANGE VINAIGRETTE

2 cups (500ml) orange juice

⅓ cup (80ml) extra virgin
   olive oil

1 teaspoon dijon mustard

1 Make orange vinaigrette.

2 Meanwhile, boil, steam or
   microwave peas until just
   tender; drain. Rinse under
   cold water; drain.

3 Combine peas in large bowl
   with mizuna, herbs and lettuce;
   drizzle salad with vinaigrette.

ORANGE VINAIGRETTE

Bring juice to a boil in medium
saucepan. Boil, uncovered, about
20 minutes or until reduced to
½ cup. Combine juice in small
bowl with oil and mustard.

serves 8

HALOUMI, PROSCIUTTO AND SPINACH SALAD

PREPARATION TIME 15 MINUTES **COOKING TIME** 15 MINUTES

13 prosciutto slices (200g)
500g asparagus, trimmed
200g haloumi cheese,
   sliced thinly
2 small pears (360g), cored,
   cut into thin wedges
200g baby spinach leaves

MACADAMIA DRESSING
½ cup (75g) toasted macadamias,
   chopped coarsely
2 tablespoons sherry vinegar
¼ cup (60ml) macadamia oil

1 Preheat grill.
2 Cook prosciutto under preheated
   grill until crisp; break prosciutto
   into bite-size pieces.
3 Meanwhile, boil, steam or
   microwave asparagus until
   just tender; drain.
4 Make macadamia dressing.
5 Cook asparagus, cheese and
   pear on heated oiled grill plate
   (or grill or barbecue) until
   browned lightly.
6 Place prosciutto, asparagus,
   cheese, pear and spinach in
   large bowl with dressing; toss
   gently to combine.

MACADAMIA DRESSING
Place ingredients in screw-top jar;
shake well.

serves 8

TIP You can substitute olive oil for
the macadamia oil, if you prefer.

BALSAMIC-GLAZED BABY ONIONS

PREPARATION TIME 10 MINUTES

COOKING TIME 15 MINUTES

1 tablespoon balsamic vinegar
1 tablespoon wholegrain mustard
¼ cup (90g) honey
2 tablespoons vegetable oil
500g baby onions, halved

1 Combine vinegar, mustard and honey in small saucepan; bring to a boil. Reduce heat; simmer, uncovered, about 5 minutes or until glaze thickens.
2 Heat oil in large frying pan; cook onion, brushing constantly with glaze, stirring, until browned and cooked as desired.

serves 8

BABY CARROTS WITH ORANGE MAPLE SYRUP

PREPARATION TIME 35 MINUTES

COOKING TIME 20 MINUTES

1.6kg baby carrots
30g butter
2 teaspoons finely grated orange rind
2 tablespoons orange juice
2 tablespoons maple syrup

1 Boil, steam or microwave carrots until just tender.
2 Melt butter in large frying pan; stir rind, juice and syrup in pan until mixture boils. Reduce heat; simmer, uncovered, until syrup mixture thickens slightly. Add drained carrots to pan, stirring gently to coat in orange maple syrup.

serves 8

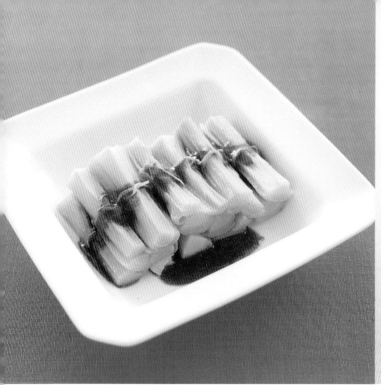

LEEKS IN VINAIGRETTE

PREPARATION TIME 20 MINUTES
COOKING TIME 35 MINUTES

4 medium leeks (1.4kg)
50g butter, chopped
⅓ cup (80ml) dry white wine
3 cups (750ml) chicken stock

RASPBERRY VINAIGRETTE
150g raspberries
¼ cup (60ml) raspberry vinegar
2 tablespoons olive oil

1 Preheat oven to moderate. Discard root end; trim green section to leave 14cm leek. Remove outer layer of each leek; cut outer layer lengthways into thin strips. Soften strips in saucepan of boiling water; drain.
2 Halve leeks crossways; quarter each piece lengthways. Tie each quarter in the centre with a few leek strips.
3 Combine butter, wine and stock in large baking dish; place leeks in stock mixture. Cook, covered, in moderate oven about 25 minutes or until leeks are tender.
4 Meanwhile, make vinaigrette; drizzle over leeks.

RASPBERRY VINAIGRETTE Push berries through sieve into small bowl; discard seeds. Whisk in vinegar and oil.

serves 8

FRESH PEAS, CARAWAY AND PARMESAN

PREPARATION TIME 35 MINUTES
COOKING TIME 5 MINUTES

You need about 1.3kg fresh peas for this recipe.

60g butter
1 teaspoon caraway seeds
2 teaspoons finely grated lemon rind
1 small red onion (100g), sliced thinly
4 cups (640g) fresh peas
⅓ cup coarsely chopped fresh flat-leaf parsley
½ cup (40g) finely grated parmesan cheese

1 Melt butter in large frying pan; cook seeds, rind and onion, stirring, until onion softens.
2 Add peas; cook, stirring, until peas are just tender. Stir in parsley; sprinkle with cheese.

serves 8

BROCCOLINI POLONAISE

PREPARATION TIME 10 MINUTES COOKING TIME 10 MINUTES

A "polonaise", the French interpretation of a classic Polish way of presenting cooked vegetables such as cauliflower, broccoli, asparagus and the like, is a topping of chopped or sieved hard-boiled egg, buttered breadcrumbs and chopped parsley.

60g butter
1 cup (70g) stale breadcrumbs
4 hard-boiled eggs,
   chopped finely
¼ cup finely chopped fresh
   flat-leaf parsley
750g broccolini
60g butter, melted

1 Melt butter in large frying pan; cook breadcrumbs, stirring, until browned and crisp. Combine breadcrumbs in small bowl with egg and parsley.
2 Boil, steam or microwave broccolini until just tender; drain.
3 Top broccolini with polonaise mixture then drizzle with the melted butter.

serves 8

WARM POTATO SALAD WITH CAPERBERRIES

PREPARATION TIME 10 MINUTES COOKING TIME 15 MINUTES

2kg pontiac potatoes, unpeeled,
   diced into 2cm pieces
1 tablespoon dijon mustard
2 tablespoons red wine vinegar
½ cup (125ml) extra virgin
   olive oil
1 small white onion (80g),
   sliced thinly
¼ cup firmly packed fresh
   flat-leaf parsley leaves
2 tablespoons fresh dill sprigs
1 cup (200g) cornichons,
   halved lengthways
½ cup (80g) drained large
   caperberries, rinsed

1 Boil, steam or microwave
   potato until just tender; drain.
2 Meanwhile, whisk mustard,
   vinegar and oil in large bowl
   until combined. Add hot potato
   to bowl with onion, herbs,
   cornichons and caperberries;
   toss gently to combine.

serves 8

SESAME PATTY-PAN SQUASH AND SUGAR SNAP PEAS

PREPARATION TIME 5 MINUTES

COOKING TIME 10 MINUTES

16 yellow patty-pan squash (480g)
300g sugar snap peas, trimmed
2 teaspoons sesame oil
1 tablespoon soy sauce
1 tablespoon toasted sesame seeds

1 Boil, steam or microwave squash and peas, separately, until tender; drain.
2 Place vegetables in large bowl with remaining ingredients; toss gently to combine.

serves 8

BARBECUED CORN, BROAD BEANS AND CAPSICUM

PREPARATION TIME 20 MINUTES

COOKING TIME 15 MINUTES

4 trimmed corn cobs (1kg)
500g frozen broad beans, thawed, peeled
1 medium red capsicum (200g), chopped finely
20g butter

1 Cook corn on heated oiled grill plate (or grill or barbecue) until just tender. When cool enough to handle, use a sharp knife to cut kernels from cobs.
2 Meanwhile, boil, steam or microwave broad beans until tender; drain.
3 Place corn and beans in large bowl with remaining ingredients; toss gently to combine.

serves 8

BABY BEETROOT WITH CAPER VINAIGRETTE

PREPARATION TIME 10 MINUTES

COOKING TIME 20 MINUTES

You need approximately two bunches of baby beetroot for this recipe.

1kg baby beetroot
1 tablespoon drained baby capers, rinsed
2 tablespoons white wine vinegar
2 tablespoons olive oil
1 teaspoon dijon mustard

1   Remove stems from beetroot; cook beetroot in large saucepan of boiling water, uncovered, about 20 minutes or until tender. Drain; cool 10 minutes. Peel beetroot.
2   Place beetroot in large bowl with remaining ingredients; toss gently to combine.

serves 8

ROASTED TRUSS TOMATOES WITH CRISPY BASIL LEAVES

PREPARATION TIME 10 MINUTES

COOKING TIME 10 MINUTES

500g baby vine-ripened truss tomatoes
2 cloves garlic, sliced thinly
1 tablespoon olive oil
2 teaspoons balsamic vinegar
vegetable oil, for deep-frying
⅓ cup loosely packed fresh basil leaves

1   Preheat oven to moderate.
2   Place tomatoes on oven tray; pour combined garlic, oil and vinegar over tomatoes. Roast, uncovered, in moderate oven about 10 minutes or until tomatoes soften.
3   Meanwhile, heat vegetable oil in small saucepan; deep-fry basil, in batches, until crisp.
4   Serve tomatoes sprinkled with basil.

serves 8

RICE NOODLE SALAD WITH WASABI DRESSING

PREPARATION TIME 15 MINUTES   COOKING TIME 10 MINUTES

375g dried rice stick noodles
100g snow pea sprouts,
  sliced thinly
2 medium carrots (240g),
  cut into matchsticks
2 cups (160g) bean sprouts
1 cup loosely packed fresh
  coriander leaves
1 medium red onion (170g),
  sliced thinly
2 lebanese cucumbers (260g),
  seeded, sliced thinly
1 medium red capsicum (200g),
  sliced thinly
1 cup (150g) toasted peanuts

WASABI DRESSING

¾ cup (180ml) lime juice
¼ cup (60ml) peanut oil
1 teaspoon sesame oil
2 tablespoons rice wine vinegar
1 tablespoon soy sauce
1 tablespoon sugar
1 tablespoon fish sauce
2 teaspoons wasabi paste

1 Place noodles in medium
   heatproof bowl, cover with
   boiling water, stand until just
   tender; drain.
2 Make wasabi dressing.
3 Place noodles in large bowl
   with remaining ingredients and
   dressing; toss gently to combine.

WASABI DRESSING Place
ingredients in screw-top jar;
shake well.

serves 8

ENDIVE, LYCHEE AND PAPAYA SALAD WITH PASSIONFRUIT DRESSING

PREPARATION TIME 15 MINUTES

We used a just-ripe red-fleshed hawaiian (also called fijian) papaya. You need approximately four passionfruit for this recipe. If fresh lychees are available, you can substitute about 10 of them for the canned variety.

3 witlof (375g)
1 small papaya (650g),
  chopped coarsely
½ cup loosely packed fresh
  mint leaves
½ cup loosely packed fresh
  thai basil leaves
2 fresh long red chillies,
  sliced thinly
150g curly endive
565g can lychees, drained

PASSIONFRUIT DRESSING
⅓ cup (80ml) passionfruit pulp
¼ cup (60ml) lemon juice
¼ cup (60ml) light olive oil

1 Cut bases from witlof; slice leaves
   thickly lengthways.
2 Make passionfruit dressing.
3 Place witlof in large bowl with
   remaining ingredients and
   dressing; toss gently to combine.

PASSIONFRUIT DRESSING
Place ingredients in screw-top jar;
shake well.

serves 8

TURKEY RILLETTES

PREPARATION TIME 15 MINUTES
COOKING TIME 5 MINUTES

Melt 100g butter with ⅓ cup cream and
¼ teaspoon hot paprika in small saucepan,
stirring over low heat, until combined. Blend or
process 2 cups (320g) coarsely chopped cooked
turkey meat, ½ coarsely chopped small red onion
and ¼ cup loosely packed fresh flat-leaf parsley
leaves, pulsing, while adding butter mixture in thin,
steady stream. Place rillette mixture in four ½-cup
(125ml) dishes, cover; refrigerate until required.
Serve with pickled onions, olives and thinly sliced
toasted french bread stick.

serves 4

VIETNAMESE TURKEY SALAD

PREPARATION TIME 20 MINUTES
COOKING TIME 2 MINUTES

Boil, steam or microwave 150g trimmed snow
peas until just tender; drain. Immediately rinse
under cold water; drain. Slice snow peas thinly
lengthways; place in large bowl with 1 seeded
lebanese cucumber cut into matchsticks, 1 medium
carrot cut into matchsticks, 1 thinly sliced small red
capsicum, 100g snow pea tendrils, ½ cup loosely
packed fresh mint leaves, ½ cup loosely packed
fresh coriander leaves and 2 cups (320g) thinly
sliced turkey meat. Place 2 tablespoons peanut
oil, 2 tablespoons lime juice, 1 tablespoon brown
sugar and 1 tablespoon fish sauce in screw-top
jar; shake well. Drizzle dressing over salad; toss
gently to combine, sprinkle with 2 tablespoons
coarsely chopped unsalted roasted peanuts.

serves 4

HAM AND EGG SLICE

PREPARATION TIME 15 MINUTES
COOKING TIME 35 MINUTES

Preheat oven to moderately slow. Oil and line base of 20cm x 30cm lamington pan. Heat 2 teaspoons olive oil in medium frying pan; cook 2 thinly sliced medium brown onions and 2 cloves crushed garlic, stirring, until onion softens. Cool 5 minutes. Combine onion mixture in large bowl with 2 cups (360g) finely chopped cooked ham, 6 eggs, 300ml cream, ½ cup finely grated parmesan cheese and ¼ cup finely chopped fresh basil; pour mixture into prepared pan. Bake, uncovered, in moderately slow oven about 30 minutes or until set.

serves 8

SALMON, PEA AND MINT BAVETTE

PREPARATION TIME 10 MINUTES
COOKING TIME 15 MINUTES

Cook 375g bavette (or any long flat pasta) in large saucepan of boiling water, uncovered, until just tender. Meanwhile, cook 1 finely chopped medium brown onion and 1 clove crushed garlic in oiled large frying pan until onion softens. Add ½ cup chicken stock, ½ cup water and ¼ cup dry white wine, reduce heat; simmer, uncovered, until liquid reduces by one third. Add 1 cup (120g) frozen peas, 2 cups (400g) flaked cooked salmon and ⅓ cup coarsely chopped fresh mint; stir until just heated through. Add to drained pasta; toss gently to combine.

serves 4

GOAT CHEESE AND ROAST VEGIE TART

PREPARATION TIME 15 MINUTES
COOKING TIME 20 MINUTES

Preheat oven to very hot. Line oven tray with baking paper. Place 1 ready-rolled butter puff pastry sheet on prepared tray; spread with 2 cloves crushed garlic, sprinkle with 2 tablespoons fresh oregano leaves. Top with 3 cups (500g) coarsely chopped roasted vegetables, 1 coarsely chopped medium egg tomato and 150g crumbled goat cheese. Bake, uncovered, in very hot oven about 20 minutes or until pastry is browned lightly; sprinkle with 1 tablespoon fresh oregano leaves.

serves 4

TURKEY SALAD SANDWICHES

PREPARATION TIME 15 MINUTES

Combine 1 cup (150g) finely chopped cooked turkey meat, 1 finely chopped trimmed celery stalk, 30g finely chopped baby rocket leaves, 2 tablespoons coarsely chopped toasted slivered almonds, ¼ cup sour cream, ¼ cup whole-egg mayonnaise and 1 tablespoon lemon juice in small bowl. Spread turkey mixture over four slices of wholemeal bread; top with another four slices of wholemeal bread.

makes 4

CHRISTMAS CAKE ICE-CREAM TERRINE

PREPARATION TIME 15 MINUTES
(PLUS FREEZING TIME)

Line 14cm x 21cm loaf pan with plastic wrap.
Cut 450g Christmas cake into 1.5cm slices;
brush cake slices with 2 tablespoons Cointreau.
Stir 1 tablespoon finely grated orange rind into
2 litres softened good-quality vanilla ice-cream.
Spread half of the ice-cream mixture into prepared
pan; top with cake slices then remaining ice-cream.
Cover with plastic wrap; freeze until firm. Using hot
knife, cut terrine into six slices.

serves 6

CHRISTMAS CAKE CREAM PARFAITS

PREPARATION TIME 20 MINUTES

Combine 250g mascarpone, 2 tablespoons
whisky and 1 tablespoon icing sugar mixture
in large bowl. Beat ½ cup thickened cream in
small bowl until soft peaks form; fold cream
mixture into mascarpone mixture. Layer
1 cup (150g) crumbled Christmas cake in
base of six ¾-cup (180ml) glasses; sprinkle
½ teaspoon whisky over cake in each glass.
Divide half of the mascarpone mixture among
glasses. Repeat process with another 1 cup
(150g) crumbled Christmas cake, 2 teaspoons
whisky and remaining mascarpone mixture.
Cover; refrigerate until required. Serve topped
with raspberries and sifted icing sugar, if desired.

serves 6

GINGER AND LIME CAKE

PREPARATION TIME 45 MINUTES

COOKING TIME 45 MINUTES (PLUS REFRIGERATION TIME)

This cake is best made the day before required to allow for easy cutting. You need about eight limes for this recipe.

250g butter, chopped
½ cup (110g) firmly packed
    dark brown sugar
⅔ cup (230g) golden syrup
12cm piece fresh ginger (60g), grated
¾ cup (180ml) thickened cream
2 eggs
1 cup (150g) plain flour
1 cup (150g) self-raising flour
½ teaspoon bicarbonate of soda
1 cup (50g) flaked coconut

LIME SYRUP

½ cup (125ml) lime juice
½ cup (125ml) water
½ cup (110g) caster sugar

MASCARPONE CREAM

250g mascarpone cheese
300ml thickened cream
2 tablespoons icing sugar mixture
2 teaspoons finely grated lime rind

1 Preheat oven to moderate. Grease deep 22cm-round cake pan; line base and side with baking paper.

2 Melt butter in medium saucepan; add brown sugar, golden syrup and ginger. Stir over medium heat until sugar dissolves.

3 Whisk in cream, eggs and combined sifted flours and soda. Pour mixture into prepared pan; bake, uncovered, in moderate oven about 40 minutes.

4 Meanwhile, make lime syrup.

5 Pierce hot cake, still in pan, all over with skewer; drizzle hot lime syrup over cake. Cover; refrigerate about 3 hours or until cold.

6 Meanwhile, make mascarpone cream.

7 Remove cake from pan; line base and side of same cleaned pan with plastic wrap. Split cake into three layers; return one layer of cake to prepared pan. Spread layer with 1 cup of the mascarpone cream; repeat with second cake layer and 1 cup of the remaining mascarpone cream, top with third cake layer. Cover; refrigerate 2 hours. Refrigerate remaining mascarpone cream, covered, until required.

8 Remove cake from pan, spread remaining mascarpone cream around side and top of cake; press coconut onto sides of cake.

LIME SYRUP Stir ingredients in small saucepan over heat, without boiling, until sugar dissolves; bring to a boil. Reduce heat; simmer, uncovered, without stirring, 2 minutes. Strain into small heatproof jug.

MASCARPONE CREAM Whisk ingredients in small bowl until soft peaks form. Refrigerate until required.

serves 8

GOURMET CHOCOLATE TART

PREPARATION TIME 40 MINUTES (PLUS REFRIGERATION TIME) **COOKING TIME** 30 MINUTES

2 eggs
2 egg yolks
¼ cup (55g) caster sugar
250g dark eating chocolate, melted
200g butter, melted

TART SHELL

1½ cups (225g) plain flour
½ cup (110g) caster sugar
140g cold butter, chopped
1 egg, beaten lightly

1 Make tart shell, baking in moderately hot oven as instructed below then reducing oven temperature to moderate.
2 Whisk eggs, egg yolks and sugar in medium heatproof bowl over medium saucepan of simmering water about 15 minutes or until light and fluffy. Gently whisk chocolate and butter into egg mixture.
3 Pour mixture into shell. Bake, uncovered, in moderate oven about 10 minutes or until filling is set; cool 10 minutes. Refrigerate 1 hour. Serve dusted with cocoa powder, if desired.

TART SHELL Blend or process flour, sugar and butter until crumbly; add egg, process until ingredients just come together. Knead dough on floured surface until smooth. Enclose in plastic wrap; refrigerate 30 minutes. Grease 24cm-round loose-base flan tin. Roll dough between sheets of baking paper until large enough to line prepared tin. Lift dough onto tin; press into side, trim edge, prick base all over with fork. Cover; refrigerate 30 minutes. Preheat oven to moderately hot. Place tin on oven tray; cover dough with baking paper, fill with dried beans or rice. Bake, uncovered, in moderately hot oven 10 minutes. Remove paper and beans carefully from tin; bake, uncovered, in moderately hot oven about 5 minutes or until tart shell browns lightly. Cool to room temperature.

serves 8

ASIAN FRUIT SALAD

PREPARATION TIME 20 MINUTES **COOKING TIME** 15 MINUTES (PLUS COOLING AND REFRIGERATION TIME)

You need about six medium passionfruit for this recipe.

1 litre (4 cups) water
1 cup (270g) grated palm sugar
1 vanilla bean
2cm piece fresh ginger (10g), chopped finely
3 star anise
1 tablespoon finely grated lime rind
⅓ cup (80ml) lime juice
½ cup coarsely chopped fresh
   vietnamese mint
2 large mangoes (1.2kg), chopped coarsely
3 star fruit (450g), sliced thinly
2 large oranges (600g), segmented
1 large pineapple (2kg), chopped coarsely
1 medium papaya (1kg), chopped coarsely
½ cup (125ml) passionfruit pulp
12 rambutans (500g), halved
12 lychees (300g), halved

1   Stir the water and sugar in medium saucepan over high heat until sugar dissolves; bring to a boil. Reduce heat; simmer without stirring, uncovered, 5 minutes. Split vanilla bean in half lengthways; scrape seeds into pan. Add pod, ginger and star anise; simmer, uncovered, about 10 minutes or until syrup thickens. Discard pod; cool to room temperature. Stir in rind, juice and mint.
2   Combine remaining ingredients in large bowl. Pour syrup over fruit; stir gently to combine. Refrigerate fruit salad, covered, until cold.

serves 8

WHITE CHOCOLATE AND PISTACHIO PARFAIT

PREPARATION TIME 30 MINUTES

COOKING TIME 10 MINUTES (PLUS REFRIGERATION AND FREEZING TIME)

1 Combine cream and chocolate in medium saucepan; stir over low heat until smooth. Beat yolks, eggs and sugar in small bowl with electric mixer until thick and creamy; with motor operating, gradually beat hot chocolate mixture into egg mixture. Transfer parfait mixture to large bowl, cover; refrigerate about 30 minutes or until mixture thickens slightly.

2 Meanwhile, cut eight 30cm squares of baking paper; fold one square in half diagonally. Place triangle on bench with centre point towards you; curl one point towards you, turning it under where it meets the centre point. Hold these two points together with one hand then roll remaining point towards you to meet the other two, turning it under to form a cone. Staple or tape the cone securely to hold its shape; stand cone upright in tall glass. Repeat with remaining paper squares, standing each in a tall glass; place glasses on tray.

3 Beat extra cream in small bowl with electric mixer until soft peaks form; fold extra cream, liqueur and nuts into parfait mixture. Divide mixture among cones. Cover cones loosely with plastic wrap; freeze overnight.

4 Make berry compote.

5 Place parfaits on individual serving plates; carefully remove and discard paper from each. Serve with berry compote.

BERRY COMPOTE Combine ingredients in small saucepan; stir over low heat until sugar dissolves. Cool 10 minutes.

serves 8

¾ cup (180ml) thickened cream
250g white eating chocolate, chopped coarsely
6 egg yolks
2 eggs
½ cup (110g) caster sugar
1⅔ cups (400ml) thickened cream, extra
½ cup (125ml) irish cream liqueur
1 cup (150g) toasted shelled pistachios, chopped finely

BERRY COMPOTE

300g frozen mixed berries
2 tablespoons caster sugar
1 tablespoon water

Fold paper square into a triangle then roll one point over to meet centre point.

Twist second point over to meet other two points and form a cone shape.

Staple or tape the paper cones securely to ensure that they hold their shape.

VERY-BERRY PAVLOVA

PREPARATION TIME 20 MINUTES
COOKING TIME 25 MINUTES (PLUS COOLING AND REFRIGERATION TIME)

6 egg whites
1 cup (220g) caster sugar
1 tablespoon cornflour
600ml thickened cream
⅓ cup (75g) caster sugar, extra
300g fresh blueberries
360g fresh raspberries
250g strawberries, sliced thinly
2 tablespoons icing sugar mixture

MIXED BERRY COULIS

120g fresh blueberries
120g fresh raspberries
120g fresh blackberries
¼ cup (55g) caster sugar

1. Preheat oven to moderate. Grease three oven trays, line with baking paper; mark a 23cm-diameter circle on each piece of paper.
2. Beat egg whites in medium bowl with electric mixer until soft peaks form. Add sugar, 1 tablespoon at a time, beating until sugar dissolves between each addition; beat in cornflour.
3. Spread meringue over circles on prepared trays; bake, uncovered, in moderate oven 10 minutes. Reduce temperature to slow; bake 15 minutes. Cool meringues in oven with door ajar.
4. Meanwhile, make mixed berry coulis.
5. Beat cream and extra sugar in small bowl with electric mixer until firm peaks form.
6. Place one meringue on serving plate; flatten slightly. Layer with half of the cream mixture then top with half of the combined berries. Repeat layering with a second meringue, remaining cream and three-quarters of remaining berries, reserving remaining berries for garnish. Cover pavlova; refrigerate 3 hours.
7. Top pavlova with reserved berries, dust with sifted icing sugar; serve with coulis.

MIXED BERRY COULIS Combine ingredients in medium saucepan, simmer, uncovered, over low heat, about 10 minutes or until berries have softened. Push coulis mixture through sieve into medium bowl; cool. Discard seeds.

serves 8

FRUIT CAKE 'N' EGGNOG CHEESECAKE

PREPARATION TIME 25 MINUTES (PLUS COOLING AND REFRIGERATION TIME)
COOKING TIME 55 MINUTES

350g fruit cake, cut into 1cm slices
750g packaged cream cheese, softened
300g sour cream
1 teaspoon vanilla extract
¼ cup (60ml) brandy
½ teaspoon ground nutmeg
2 cups (440g) caster sugar
3 eggs
1 cup (250ml) water
1 medium pink grapefruit (425g), segmented
1 large orange (300g), segmented
150g strawberries, halved
100g red seedless grapes
1 large kiwifruit (100g), cut into
    eight wedges

1 Preheat oven to moderate. Line base of
   22cm springform tin with baking paper.
2 Cover base of prepared tin with cake slices.
   Bake, uncovered, in moderate oven about
   10 minutes or until browned lightly. Reduce
   oven temperature to slow.
3 Meanwhile, beat cream cheese, sour cream,
   extract, brandy, nutmeg and half of the sugar
   in medium bowl with electric mixer until
   smooth. Beat in eggs, one at a time, beat
   only until combined between each addition.
4 Pour mixture into tin. Bake, uncovered, in
   slow oven about 45 minutes or until just set.
   Cool cheesecake in oven with door ajar.
   Cover; refrigerate overnight.
5 Stir remaining sugar and the water in
   medium heavy-based frying pan over high
   heat until sugar dissolves; bring to a boil.
   Reduce heat; simmer, without stirring,
   uncovered, about 10 minutes or until toffee
   mixture is golden brown in colour. Remove
   from heat; stand until bubbles subside.
6 Meanwhile, remove cheesecake from tin,
   place on serving plate; top with fruit.
7 Working quickly, drizzle toffee over fruit.

serves 10

PASSIONFRUIT CURD TARTLETS

PREPARATION TIME 50 MINUTES (PLUS REFRIGERATING TIME)
COOKING TIME 40 MINUTES (PLUS COOLING TIME)

You need approximately 12 medium passionfruit for this recipe, as well as eight 10cm-round loose-base flan tins.

4 egg yolks
½ cup (110g) caster sugar
80g butter, softened
1 cup (250ml) passionfruit pulp
1 teaspoon gelatine
2 tablespoons water
½ cup (125ml) cream

TARTLET SHELLS

1⅔ cups (250g) plain flour
½ cup (110g) caster sugar
140g cold butter, chopped
1 egg, beaten lightly
2 teaspoons iced water, approximately

BERRY TOPPING

¼ cup (80g) raspberry jam
1 tablespoon water
150g blueberries

1 Make tartlet shells, baking in moderate oven as instructed below.
2 Meanwhile, combine yolks, sugar, butter and ⅓ cup of the pulp in medium heatproof bowl. Place bowl over medium saucepan of simmering water; cook, stirring, about 15 minutes or until curd coats the back of a spoon. Strain; discard seeds.
3 Sprinkle gelatine over the water in small heatproof jug. Stand jug in small saucepan of simmering water; stir until gelatine dissolves. Stir gelatine mixture and remaining pulp into warm curd, cover; refrigerate 1 hour.
4 Meanwhile, make berry topping.
5 Beat cream in small bowl until soft peaks form; fold cream into curd mixture. Divide curd filling among tartlet shells; refrigerate until firm. Serve tartlets with berry topping.

TARTLET SHELLS Blend or process flour, sugar and butter until crumbly; add egg and enough of the water to make ingredients just come together. Knead dough on floured surface until smooth, enclose in plastic wrap; refrigerate 30 minutes. Divide dough into eight portions; roll portions, one at a time, between floured sheets of baking paper, into rounds large enough to line eight 10cm-round loose-base flan tins. Lift rounds into tins; press into sides, trim edges, prick bases all over with fork. Cover; refrigerate 20 minutes. Preheat oven to moderate. Place tins on oven tray; line each with baking paper then fill with dried beans or uncooked rice. Bake, uncovered, in moderate oven 15 minutes. Remove paper and beans carefully from tins; bake, uncovered, in moderate oven about 7 minutes or until tartlet shells are browned lightly. Cool 10 minutes.
BERRY TOPPING Combine jam and the water in small saucepan over medium heat; simmer, stirring, until mixture reduces by half. Push jam mixture through sieve; stir blueberries gently into jam mixture.

makes 8

TIP Uncooked rice or dried beans used to weight pastry during blind-baking are not suitable for eating. You can use them every time you blind-bake; cool before storing in an airtight jar.

TRIO OF SORBETS

LEMON LIME

PREPARATION TIME 20 MINUTES
COOKING TIME 10 MINUTES
(PLUS FREEZING TIME)

2 tablespoons finely grated
   lemon rind
1 tablespoon finely grated
   lime rind
1 cup (220g) caster sugar
2½ cups (625ml) water
½ cup (125ml) lemon juice
¼ cup (60ml) lime juice
1 egg white

1   Stir rinds, sugar and the water
    in medium saucepan over high
    heat until sugar dissolves; bring
    to a boil. Reduce heat; simmer
    without stirring, uncovered,
    5 minutes. Transfer to large
    heatproof jug, cool to room
    temperature; stir in juices.
2   Pour sorbet mixture into loaf
    pan, cover tightly with foil;
    freeze 3 hours or overnight.
3   Process mixture with egg white
    until smooth. Return to loaf pan,
    cover; freeze until firm.

serves 8

PASSIONFRUIT

PREPARATION TIME 20 MINUTES
COOKING TIME 10 MINUTES
(PLUS FREEZING TIME)

**You need about 12 medium
passionfruit for this recipe.**

1 cup (250ml) passionfruit pulp
1 cup (220g) caster sugar
2½ cups (625ml) water
¼ cup (60ml) lemon juice
2 egg whites

1   Strain pulp into small bowl.
    Reserve seeds and juice.
2   Stir sugar and the water in
    medium saucepan over high
    heat until sugar dissolves; bring
    to a boil. Reduce heat; simmer
    without stirring, uncovered,
    5 minutes. Transfer to large
    heatproof jug, cool to room
    temperature; stir in lemon juice
    and passionfruit juice.
3   Pour sorbet mixture into loaf
    pan, cover tightly with foil;
    freeze 3 hours or overnight.
4   Process mixture with egg whites
    until smooth; stir in reserved
    seeds. Return to loaf pan, cover;
    freeze until firm.

serves 8

RASPBERRY

PREPARATION TIME 20 MINUTES
COOKING TIME 10 MINUTES
(PLUS FREEZING TIME)

360g raspberries
1 cup (220g) caster sugar
2½ cups (625ml) water
1 tablespoon lemon juice
1 egg white

1   Press raspberries through sieve
    into small bowl; discard seeds.
2   Stir sugar and the water in
    medium saucepan over high
    heat until sugar dissolves; bring
    to a boil. Reduce heat; simmer
    without stirring, uncovered,
    5 minutes. Transfer to large
    heatproof jug, cool to room
    temperature; stir in raspberry
    pulp and lemon juice.
3   Pour sorbet mixture into loaf
    pan, cover tightly with foil;
    freeze 3 hours or overnight.
4   Process mixture with egg white
    until smooth. Return to loaf pan,
    cover; freeze until firm.

serves 8

THREE-IN-ONE CHRISTMAS MIX

One quantity of this basic fruit mixture recipe makes enough for all three of these Christmas recipes. The mixture can be made a month before required, and stored in a cool, dark place – your refrigerator is ideal. Ideally, the ingredients shown below as "chopped" should all be cut to a similar size, about that of a sultana. Grand Marnier liqueur was used in keeping with the citrus content of the mixture (you can use any citrus-flavoured liqueur), but it can be substituted with rum, sherry or brandy.

BASIC FRUIT MIXTURE

PREPARATION TIME 45 MINUTES (PLUS STANDING TIME)

6 cups (1kg) sultanas
2½ cups (375g) dried currants
2¼ cups (425g) raisins, chopped
1½ cups (250g) seeded dried
   dates, chopped
1½ cups (250g) seeded prunes, chopped
1¼ cups (250g) glacé cherries, quartered
½ cup (125g) glacé apricots, chopped
½ cup (115g) glacé pineapple, chopped
½ cup (115g) glacé ginger, chopped
¾ cup (120g) mixed peel
3 medium apples (450g), peeled, grated
⅔ cup (240g) fig jam
2 tablespoons finely grated orange rind
¼ cup (60ml) lemon juice
2 cups (440g) firmly packed brown sugar
1 tablespoon mixed spice
1⅓ cups (330ml) Grand Marnier

1 Mix ingredients in large bowl; cover tightly with plastic wrap. Store mixture in cool, dark place for a month (or longer, if desired) before using; stir mixture every two or three days.

CHRISTMAS PUDDING

PREPARATION TIME 15 MINUTES
COOKING TIME 4 HOURS (PLUS STANDING TIME)

You need a 60cm square of unbleached calico for the pudding cloth. If calico has not been used before, soak in cold water overnight; next day, boil it for 20 minutes then rinse in cold water.

¼ quantity basic fruit mixture
250g butter, melted, cooled
3 eggs, beaten lightly
4 cups (280g) stale breadcrumbs
¼ cup (35g) plain flour

1 Place basic fruit mixture in large bowl. Mix in butter and eggs then breadcrumbs and the flour.
2 Fill large boiler three-quarters full of hot water, cover; bring to a boil. Have ready 2.5 metres of kitchen string and an extra ½ cup of plain flour. Wearing thick rubber gloves, put pudding cloth in boiling water; boil 1 minute; squeeze excess water from cloth. Working quickly, spread hot cloth on bench, rub flour into centre of cloth to cover an area about 40cm in diameter, leaving flour a little thicker in centre of cloth where "skin" on the pudding needs to be thickest.
3 Place pudding mixture in centre of cloth. Gather cloth evenly around mixture, avoiding any deep pleats; then pat into round shape. Tie cloth tightly with string as close to mixture as possible. Pull ends of cloth tightly to ensure pudding is as round and firm as possible. Knot two pairs of corners together to make pudding easier to remove.
4 Lower pudding into boiling water; tie free ends of string to handles of boiler to suspend pudding. Cover with tight-fitting lid; boil rapidly for 4 hours, replenishing water as necessary to maintain level.
5 Untie pudding from handles; place wooden spoon through knotted calico loops to lift pudding from water. Do not put pudding on bench; suspend from spoon by placing over rungs of upturned stool or wedging handle in a drawer. Pudding must be suspended freely. Twist wet ends of cloth around string to avoid them touching pudding. If pudding has been cooked correctly, cloth will start to dry in patches within a few minutes; hang 10 minutes.
6 Place pudding on board; cut string, carefully peel back cloth. Turn pudding onto a plate then carefully peel cloth away completely; cool. Stand at least 20 minutes or until skin darkens and pudding becomes firm.

TIP For tips on how to store and reheat your pudding, see page 94.

MOIST CHRISTMAS CAKE

PREPARATION TIME 15 MINUTES **COOKING TIME** 3 HOURS (PLUS COOLING TIME)

½ quantity basic fruit mixture
(page 82)
250g butter, melted, cooled
5 eggs, beaten lightly
2½ cups (375g) plain flour
2 tablespoons Grand Marnier

1 Preheat oven to slow. Line
base and sides of deep
22cm-square cake pan with
one thickness brown paper
and two thicknesses baking
paper, extending papers 5cm
above sides of pan.
2 Place basic fruit mixture in large
bowl. Mix in butter and eggs
then sifted flour in two batches.
3 Spread mixture into prepared
pan; level top with spatula. Bake,
uncovered, in slow oven about
3 hours. Brush with liqueur;
cover hot cake in pan with foil,
cool overnight.

TIP Can be made three months
ahead and stored in an airtight
container under refrigeration.

FRUIT MINCE SLICE

PREPARATION TIME 10 MINUTES **COOKING TIME** 25 MINUTES

2 sheets ready-rolled puff pastry
¼ quantity basic fruit mixture
   (page 82)
1 egg white, beaten lightly
1 tablespoon caster sugar

1 Preheat oven to hot. Grease 20cm x 30cm lamington pan.

2 Cut one pastry sheet large enough to cover base of prepared pan. Using fork, prick pastry all over several times. Place 19cm x 29cm slice pan on top of pastry to prevent pastry rising during cooking.

3 Bake pastry in hot oven about 10 minutes or until pastry is browned lightly and crisp.

4 Remove slice pan; spread fruit mixture evenly over pastry.

5 Cut remaining pastry sheet large enough to cover fruit mixture. Brush pastry with egg white, sprinkle with sugar; carefully score pastry in crosshatch pattern. Bake, uncovered, in hot oven about 15 minutes or until pastry is browned. Serve slice with custard, if desired.

GRAND MARNIER FRUIT CAKE

PREPARATION TIME 2 HOURS (PLUS STANDING TIME) **COOKING TIME** 3 HOURS 40 MINUTES (PLUS COOLING TIME)

3 cups (500g) sultanas

1½ cups (250g) mixed peel

¾ cup (120g) coarsely
chopped raisins

¾ cup (120g) coarsely chopped
seeded dried dates

⅔ cup (140g) coarsely chopped
seeded prunes

½ cup (125g) coarsely chopped
glacé apricots

⅔ cup (150g) coarsely
chopped glacé pineapple

½ cup (70g) slivered almonds

½ cup (60g) coarsely
chopped walnuts

1 tablespoon finely grated
orange rind

½ cup (110g) caster sugar

¼ cup (60ml) orange juice

½ cup (125ml) Grand Marnier

250g butter, softened

½ cup (110g) firmly packed
brown sugar

5 eggs

2 cups (300g) plain flour

2 tablespoons Grand Marnier, extra

1kg ready-made fondant

1 egg white, beaten lightly

½ cup (80g) pure icing
sugar, sifted

25cm-round covered cake board

decorative ribbon

13g packet silver cachous

1 Combine fruit, nuts and rind in large bowl. Cook caster sugar in large frying pan over low heat, without stirring, until it begins to melt then stir until sugar is melted and browned lightly. Remove from heat, slowly stir in juice; return to low heat, stir until toffee dissolves (do not boil). Add liqueur; pour over fruit mixture, cover tightly with plastic wrap. Store mixture in cool, dark place for 10 days, stirring every day.

2 Preheat oven to slow. Line base and sides of deep 22cm-round or deep 19cm-square cake pan with one thickness of brown paper and two thicknesses of baking paper, extending papers 5cm above edge.

3 Beat butter and brown sugar in small bowl with electric mixer until just combined; beat in eggs, one at a time, until just combined between additions. Stir butter mixture into fruit mixture, mix in flour; spread mixture into prepared pan. Tap pan firmly on bench to settle mixture into pan; level cake mixture with wet spatula.

4 Bake cake, uncovered, in slow oven 3½ hours. Remove cake from oven, brush with extra liqueur; cover hot cake with foil then turn upside down to cool overnight.

5 Trim top of cake with sharp knife to ensure it sits flat when turned upside down. Mix a little fondant and cold boiled water to a sticky paste. Spread about 2 tablespoons of this mixture into the centre of a sheet of baking paper about 5cm larger than the cake; position cake upside down on paper.

6 Using spatula and small pieces of fondant, patch any holes on cake.

7 Brush egg white evenly over cake. Knead fondant on surface dusted with icing sugar until smooth; roll to 7mm thickness. Lift fondant onto cake with rolling pin, smoothing fondant all over cake with hands dusted with icing sugar. Using sharp knife, cut excess fondant away from base of cake.

8 Mix scraps of fondant and cold boiled water to a sticky paste. Spread about 2 tablespoons of paste in centre of board; centre cake on prepared board. Move the cake to the correct position on the board; using sharp craft knife or scalpel, carefully cut away excess baking paper extending around base of cake.

9 Secure ribbon around cake using pins (remove to a safe place before cutting cake). Push cachous gently into fondant in the design of your choice.

Use spatula and tiny pieces of fondant to patch holes on top and side of cake.

Using rolling pin dusted with icing sugar, carefully lift fondant onto the cake.

Smooth fondant onto cake then cut away excess around base using a sharp knife.

STEAMED CHRISTMAS PUDDING

PREPARATION TIME 25 MINUTES **COOKING TIME** 4 HOURS 15 MINUTES (PLUS COOLING TIME)

3 cups (450g) chopped mixed
  dried fruit
¾ cup (120g) finely chopped
  dried seedless dates
¾ cup (120g) finely
  chopped raisins
¾ cup (180ml) water
1 cup (220g) firmly packed
  brown sugar
100g butter, chopped
1 teaspoon bicarbonate of soda
2 eggs, beaten lightly
¾ cup (110g) plain flour
¾ cup (110g) self-raising flour
1 teaspoon mixed spice
½ teaspoon ground cinnamon
2 tablespoons dark rum

1 Combine fruit, the water, sugar
   and butter in medium saucepan.
   Stir over medium heat until butter
   melts and sugar dissolves; bring
   to a boil. Reduce heat; simmer,
   uncovered, 6 minutes. Stir in
   soda. Transfer mixture to large
   bowl; cool to room temperature.
2 Stir in eggs, sifted dry ingredients
   and rum.
3 Grease 2-litre (8-cup) pudding
   steamer; spoon mixture into
   steamer. Top with pleated baking
   paper and foil (to allow pudding
   to expand as it cooks); secure
   with kitchen string or lid.
4 Place pudding in large boiler with
   enough boiling water to come
   halfway up side of steamer.
   Cover with tight-fitting lid, boil
   for 4 hours, replenishing water
   as necessary to maintain level.
   Stand pudding 10 minutes
   before turning onto plate; serve
   with cream, if desired.

TIPS To store pudding: allow pudding to come to room temperature
then wrap pudding in plastic wrap; refrigerate in cleaned steamer, or
seal tightly in freezer bag or airtight container. Pudding can be stored in
refrigerator up to two months or frozen up to 12 months.
To reheat: thaw frozen pudding three days in refrigerator; remove from
refrigerator 12 hours before reheating. Remove from plastic wrap and
return to steamer. Steam 2 hours following instructions in step 4.
To reheat in microwave oven: reheat up to four single serves at once.
Cover with plastic wrap; microwave on HIGH (100%) up to 1 minute per
serve. To reheat whole pudding, cover with plastic wrap; microwave on
MEDIUM (55%) about 15 minutes or until hot.

GLACE FRUIT AND CITRUS FROZEN PUDDINGS WITH BITTER ORANGE SAUCE

PREPARATION TIME 40 MINUTES (PLUS FREEZING TIME)

1½ cups (280g) finely chopped
   mixed glacé fruit

½ cup (170g) orange marmalade

2 tablespoons Grand Marnier

2 teaspoons finely grated
   orange rind

¼ cup coarsely chopped
   fresh mint

2 litres vanilla ice-cream,
   slightly softened

BITTER ORANGE SAUCE

⅔ cup (160ml) orange juice

⅓ cup (115g) orange
   marmalade

2 tablespoons lemon juice

1 tablespoon Grand Marnier

1 Line eight 1-cup (250ml) moulds
   with plastic wrap.
2 Combine fruit, marmalade, liqueur,
   rind and mint in medium bowl.
3 Place ice-cream in large bowl;
   fold in fruit mixture. Divide mixture
   among prepared moulds; cover
   with foil. Freeze puddings 3 hours
   or overnight.
4 Make bitter orange sauce.
5 Turn puddings out of moulds
   onto serving plates; serve with
   bitter orange sauce.

BITTER ORANGE SAUCE
Combine ingredients in small jug.

serves 8

FESTIVE FRUIT AND NUT CAKE

PREPARATION TIME 20 MINUTES

COOKING TIME 1 HOUR 45 MINUTES (PLUS STANDING TIME)

½ cup (115g) coarsely chopped
glacé pineapple

½ cup (125g) coarsely chopped
glacé apricots

1½ cups (250g) seeded
dried dates

½ cup (110g) red glacé cherries

½ cup (110g) green glacé cherries

1 cup (170g) brazil nuts

½ cup (75g) macadamia nuts

2 eggs

½ cup (110g) firmly packed
brown sugar

1 tablespoon dark rum

100g butter, melted

⅓ cup (50g) plain flour

¼ cup (35g) self-raising flour

FRUIT AND NUT TOPPING

⅓ cup (75g) coarsely chopped
glacé pineapple

¼ cup (55g) red glacé
cherries, halved

¼ cup (55g) green glacé
cherries, halved

¼ cup (40g) brazil nuts

¼ cup (35g) macadamia nuts

TOFFEE TOPPING

½ cup (110g) caster sugar

¼ cup (60ml) water

1 Preheat oven to slow.

2 Grease 20cm-ring pan; line base and side with baking paper, extending paper 5cm above side.

3 Combine fruit and nuts in large bowl.

4 Beat eggs and sugar in small bowl with electric mixer until thick. Add rum, butter and sifted flours; beat until just combined. Stir egg mixture into fruit mixture. Press mixture firmly into prepared pan.

5 Make fruit and nut topping. Gently press topping evenly over cake mixture; bake, covered, in slow oven 1 hour. Uncover; bake in slow oven about 45 minutes. Stand cake in pan 10 minutes.

6 Meanwhile, make toffee topping. Turn cake, top-side up, onto wire rack; drizzle with toffee topping.

FRUIT AND NUT TOPPING Combine ingredients in medium bowl.

TOFFEE TOPPING Combine ingredients in small saucepan, stir over heat without boiling until sugar dissolves; bring to a boil. Reduce heat; simmer, uncovered, without stirring, about 10 minutes or until mixture is golden. Remove from heat; stand until bubbles subside before using.

TIP This cake can be baked in two 8cm x 26cm bar cake pans. Line bases and sides with baking paper, extending paper 5cm above long sides. Bake, covered, in slow oven 1 hour; uncover, bake in slow oven about 30 minutes.

Simmer toffee mixture, without stirring, about 10 minutes or until golden.

Turn cake, top-side up, onto wire rack; drizzle with the hot toffee topping.

CELEBRATION FRUIT CAKE

PREPARATION TIME 20 MINUTES (PLUS STANDING TIME)   **COOKING TIME** 3 HOURS 30 MINUTES (PLUS COOLING TIME)

3 cups (500g) sultanas
1¾ cups (300g) raisins, halved
1¾ cups (300g) dried dates,
   chopped finely
1 cup (150g) dried currants
⅔ cup (110g) mixed peel
⅔ cup (150g) glacé
   cherries, halved
¼ cup (55g) coarsely
   chopped glacé pineapple
¼ cup (60g) coarsely
   chopped glacé apricots
½ cup (125ml) dark rum
250g butter, softened
1 cup (220g) firmly packed
   brown sugar
5 eggs
1½ cups (225g) plain flour
⅓ cup (50g) self-raising flour
1 teaspoon mixed spice
2 tablespoons dark rum, extra

1 Combine fruit and rum in large
  bowl; mix well; cover tightly with
  plastic wrap. Store mixture in
  cool, dark place overnight or up
  to a week stirring every day.
2 Preheat oven to slow. Line deep
  22cm-round cake pan with three
  thicknesses of baking paper,
  extending paper 5cm above side.
3 Beat butter and sugar in small
  bowl with electric mixer until just
  combined. Add eggs, one at a
  time, beating only until combined
  between additions.
4 Add butter mixture to fruit
  mixture; mix well. Mix in sifted
  dry ingredients; spread mixture
  evenly into prepared pan. Bake,
  uncovered, in slow oven about
  3½ hours.
5 Brush cake with extra rum.
  Cover hot cake, in pan, tightly
  with foil; cool overnight.

LAST-MINUTE FRUIT CAKE

PREPARATION TIME 20 MINUTES **COOKING TIME** 2 HOURS (PLUS COOLING TIME)

1½ cups (240g) sultanas

1 cup (170g) raisins,
chopped coarsely

1 cup (150g) dried currants

½ cup (85g) mixed peel

⅓ cup (70g) glacé cherries, halved

2 tablespoons coarsely
chopped glacé pineapple

2 tablespoons coarsely
chopped glacé apricots

185g butter, chopped

¾ cup (165g) firmly packed
brown sugar

⅓ cup (80ml) brandy

⅓ cup (80ml) water

2 teaspoons finely grated
orange rind

1 teaspoon finely grated
lemon rind

1 tablespoon treacle

3 eggs, beaten lightly

1¼ cups (185g) plain flour

¼ cup (35g) self-raising flour

½ teaspoon bicarbonate of soda

½ cup (80g) blanched almonds

1 Line deep 20cm-round cake
pan with three thicknesses of
baking paper, extending paper
5cm above side.

2 Combine fruit, butter, sugar,
brandy and the water in medium
saucepan, stir over medium heat
until butter is melted and sugar is
dissolved; bring to a boil. Remove
from heat; transfer to large bowl.
Cool to room temperature.

3 Preheat oven to slow.

4 Stir rinds, treacle and eggs
into fruit mixture then sifted dry
ingredients. Spread mixture into
prepared pan; decorate with nuts.

5 Bake in slow oven, uncovered,
about 2 hours. Cover hot cake
with foil; cool in pan overnight.

BOILED CHRISTMAS PUDDING

PREPARATION TIME 30 MINUTES (PLUS STANDING TIME)
COOKING TIME 6 HOURS (PLUS COOLING TIME)

You need a 60cm square of unbleached calico for the pudding cloth. If calico has not been used before, soak in cold water overnight; next day, boil it for 20 minutes then rinse in cold water.

1½ cups (250g) raisins
1½ cups (240g) sultanas
1 cup (150g) dried currants
¾ cup (120g) mixed peel
1 teaspoon finely grated
  lemon rind
2 tablespoons lemon juice
2 tablespoons brandy
250g butter, softened
2 cups (440g) firmly packed
  brown sugar
5 eggs
1¼ cups (185g) plain flour
½ teaspoon ground nutmeg
½ teaspoon mixed spice
4 cups (280g) stale breadcrumbs

1 Combine fruit, rind, juice and brandy in large bowl; mix well. Cover tightly with plastic wrap; store in a cool, dark place overnight or up to a week, stirring every day.

2 Beat butter and sugar in large bowl with electric mixer only until combined. Beat in eggs, one at a time, beat only until combined between each addition. Add butter mixture to fruit mixture then sifted dry ingredients and breadcrumbs; mix well.

3 Fill large boiler three-quarters full of hot water, cover; bring to a boil. Have ready 2.5m of kitchen string and an extra ½ cup of plain flour. Wearing thick rubber gloves, dip pudding cloth in boiling water; boil 1 minute then remove, carefully squeeze excess water from cloth. Working quickly, spread hot cloth on bench, rub flour into centre of cloth to cover an area about 40cm in diameter, leaving flour a little thicker in centre of cloth where "skin" on the pudding needs to be thickest.

4 Place pudding mixture in centre of cloth. Gather cloth evenly around mixture, avoiding any deep pleats; then pat into round shape. Tie cloth tightly with string as close to mixture as possible. Pull ends of cloth tightly to ensure pudding is as round and firm as possible. Knot two pairs of corners together to make pudding easier to remove.

5 Lower pudding into boiling water; tie free ends of string to handles of boiler to suspend pudding. Cover with tight-fitting lid, boil for 6 hours, replenishing water as necessary to maintain level.

6 Untie pudding from handles; place wooden spoon through knotted calico loops to lift pudding from water. Do not put pudding on bench; suspend from spoon by placing over rungs of upturned stool or wedging handle in drawer. Pudding must be suspended freely. Twist ends of cloth around string to avoid them touching pudding. If pudding has been cooked correctly, cloth will dry in patches within a few minutes; hang 10 minutes.

7 Place pudding on board; cut string, carefully peel back cloth. Turn pudding onto a plate then carefully peel cloth away completely; cool. Stand at least 20 minutes or until skin darkens and pudding becomes firm.

TIPS **To store pudding**: after removing cloth, allow pudding to come to room temperature then wrap it in plastic wrap and seal tightly in a freezer bag or airtight container. Pudding can be stored in refrigerator up to two months or frozen up to 12 months.

To reheat: thaw frozen pudding three days in refrigerator; remove from refrigerator 12 hours before reheating. Remove plastic wrap; tie dry unfloured cloth around pudding. Boil 2 hours, following instructions in step 5. Hang hot pudding 10 minutes. Remove cloth; stand at least 20 minutes or until skin darkens before serving.

To reheat in microwave oven: reheat up to four single serves at once. Cover with plastic wrap; microwave on HIGH (100%) up to 1 minute per serve. To reheat whole pudding, cover with plastic wrap; microwave on MEDIUM (55%) about 15 minutes or until hot.

GLACE FRUIT SLICE WITH LIMONCELLO CREAM

PREPARATION TIME 30 MINUTES

COOKING TIME 45 MINUTES (PLUS REFRIGERATION TIME)

1 Preheat oven to moderately slow. Line 20cm x 30cm lamington pan with baking paper, extending paper 3cm over long sides.
2 Beat butter, rind and sugar in small bowl with electric mixer until light and fluffy. Add eggs, one at a time, beating well between additions. Mixture may curdle at this stage, but will come together later.
3 Transfer mixture to large bowl; stir in sifted flours, milk, fruit and nuts. Spread mixture into prepared pan. Bake, uncovered, in moderately slow oven about 45 minutes.
4 Meanwhile, make lemon syrup.
5 Remove slice from oven; pour hot syrup over hot slice in pan. Cover; refrigerate overnight.
6 Make limoncello cream.
7 Cut slice into small squares; serve with limoncello cream.

LEMON SYRUP Stir ingredients in small saucepan over heat, without boiling, until sugar dissolves; bring to a boil. Reduce heat; simmer, uncovered, without stirring, about 10 minutes or until thickened slightly.

LIMONCELLO CREAM Beat ingredients in small bowl with electric mixer until soft peaks form.

An Italian lemon-flavoured liqueur, limoncello was originally made from the juice and peel of lemons grown along the coast of Amalfi. You can substitute it in this recipe, if you wish, with any lemon-flavoured liqueur or with an orange-flavoured one such as Cointreau. You need approximately five lemons for this recipe.

90g butter, softened
1 tablespoon finely grated lemon rind
¾ cup (165g) caster sugar
2 eggs
¾ cup (110g) plain flour
½ cup (75g) self-raising flour
⅓ cup (80ml) milk
⅔ cup (150g) coarsely chopped glacé pineapple
⅔ cup (170g) coarsely chopped glacé apricots
⅔ cup (170g) coarsely chopped glacé peaches
¾ cup (110g) coarsely chopped dried pears
¾ cup (110g) toasted shelled pistachios

LEMON SYRUP
½ cup (125ml) lemon juice
1 cup (220g) caster sugar

LIMONCELLO CREAM
300ml thickened cream
2 tablespoons limoncello

IRISH PUDDING CAKE

PREPARATION TIME 25 MINUTES (PLUS STANDING TIME)
COOKING TIME 3 HOURS (PLUS COOLING TIME)

If your dilemma is whether to make a Christmas cake or pudding, this recipe is the best of both possible worlds because it's just as delicious served hot as a pudding or cold as a cake. And it's not necessary to make it ages in advance: starting to prepare it a day or so ahead is just fine. It will keep, covered, in the refrigerator for up to a month. Although the inclusion of Irish whiskey makes it authentic, scotch, dark rum or brandy are fine substitutes.

1½ cups (250g) seeded dried
   dates, chopped coarsely
1¼ cups (200g) seeded prunes,
   chopped coarsely
1½ cups (250g) raisins,
   chopped coarsely
1 cup (150g) dried currants
¾ cup (125g) sultanas
1 large apple (200g),
   grated coarsely
1½ cups (375ml) Irish whiskey
1¼ cups (275g) firmly packed
   dark brown sugar
185g butter, softened
3 eggs, beaten lightly
½ cup (50g) hazelnut meal
1½ cups (225g) plain flour
1 teaspoon ground nutmeg
½ teaspoon ground ginger
½ teaspoon ground cloves
½ teaspoon bicarbonate of soda

1 Combine fruit and 1 cup of the whiskey in large bowl, cover tightly with plastic wrap; stand at room temperature overnight.

2 Preheat oven to very slow. Line deep 20cm-round cake pan with two thicknesses of baking paper, extending paper 5cm above side.

3 Combine remaining whiskey and ½ cup of the sugar in small saucepan. Stir over heat until sugar dissolves; bring to a boil. Remove from heat; cool syrup 20 minutes.

4 Meanwhile, beat butter and remaining sugar in small bowl with electric mixer until just combined (do not overbeat). Add eggs, one at a time, beating until just combined between additions. Add butter mixture to fruit mixture; stir in hazelnut meal, sifted combined dry ingredients and ½ cup of the cooled syrup.

5 Spread mixture into prepared pan. Bake, uncovered, in very slow oven about 3 hours. Brush cake with reheated remaining syrup, cover with foil; cool cake in pan.

FROZEN CHOCOLATE FRUIT CAKE PUDDING

PREPARATION TIME 40 MINUTES (PLUS STANDING, REFRIGERATION AND FREEZING TIME)

COOKING TIME 10 MINUTES

1 Combine fruit, rind and brandy in large bowl; mix well. Cover tightly with plastic wrap; store in a cool, dark place overnight or up to a week, stirring every day.

2 Line 17.5cm, 1.75-litre (7-cup) pudding basin with plastic wrap, extending plastic 5cm over edge of basin.

3 Melt butter in medium saucepan, add flour; stir over heat until bubbling. Remove from heat; stir in sugar then milk and half of the cream. Stir over medium heat until mixture boils and thickens. Transfer to large bowl; stir in spread, spices and yolks. Cover surface of mixture with plastic wrap; refrigerate 1 hour.

4 Stir in fruit mixture, nuts and chopped chocolate. Beat remaining cream in small bowl with electric mixer until soft peaks form, fold into pudding mixture. Spoon mixture into prepared basin, tap basin lightly to remove air bubbles. Cover with foil; freeze 3 hours or overnight.

5 Turn pudding onto tray; remove plastic wrap, return pudding to freezer.

6 Cut a 35cm circle from a piece of paper to use as a guide; cover paper with plastic wrap. Spread melted chocolate over plastic wrap then quickly drape plastic, chocolate-side down, over pudding. Quickly smooth with hands, avoiding deep pleats in the plastic. Freeze until firm. Peel away plastic; trim away excess chocolate. Serve with a selection of fresh and frosted seasonal fruit, if desired.

½ cup (95g) coarsely chopped dried figs

¼ cup (40g) coarsely chopped raisins

¼ cup (50g) coarsely chopped dried prunes

¼ cup (60g) coarsely chopped glacé cherries

4 fresh dates (100g), seeded, chopped coarsely

2 teaspoons finely grated orange rind

½ cup (125ml) brandy

125g butter

½ cup (75g) plain flour

½ cup (110g) firmly packed brown sugar

1 cup (250ml) milk

600ml thickened cream

⅔ cup (220g) chocolate hazelnut spread

1 teaspoon ground nutmeg

1 teaspoon ground cinnamon

4 egg yolks

⅓ cup (50g) toasted hazelnuts, chopped coarsely

200g dark eating chocolate, chopped finely

200g dark eating chocolate, melted, extra

GINGERBREAD HOUSE

PREPARATION TIME 2 HOURS 30 MINUTES (PLUS REFRIGERATION TIME)
COOKING TIME 45 MINUTES (PLUS STANDING TIME)

You need thin cardboard or thick paper to make patterns for the house. The house can be assembled three days ahead.

4½ cups (675g) self-raising flour
3 teaspoons ground ginger
2 teaspoons ground cinnamon
1½ teaspoons ground clove
1 teaspoon ground nutmeg
185g butter, chopped
1 cup (220g) firmly packed dark
    brown sugar
½ cup (180g) treacle
2 eggs, beaten lightly
35cm round or square board
assorted lollies

ROYAL ICING
2 egg whites
3 cups (480g) pure icing sugar

ROYAL ICING Beat egg whites in small bowl with electric mixer until frothy; gradually beat in sifted icing sugar. Cover icing with damp cloth while not using.

TIPS You can fill the house with lollies before putting on the roof. We used mint leaves, bullets, M & M's, mini M & M's, freckles, chocolate-covered sultanas and chocolate Melts for our gingerbread house.

1 Process flour, spices and butter until mixture is crumbly (you may have to process in two batches). Add sugar, treacle and enough egg for mixture to just combine. Turn dough onto floured surface; knead until smooth. Cover; refrigerate 1 hour.

2 Meanwhile, cut paper patterns for gingerbread house: cut two 12cm x 19cm rectangles for roof; two 10.5cm x 16cm rectangles for side walls of house; and two 16cm x 18cm rectangles for front and back walls of house. Trim front and back walls to form two 11cm-high gables.

3 Preheat oven to moderate. Roll dough between sheets of baking paper until 5mm thick. Peel away top layer of paper; use patterns to cut shapes from dough. Pull away excess dough; slide baking paper with shapes onto oven tray; bake, uncovered, in moderate oven about 12 minutes or until shapes are just firm (they become crisp after they cool). Re-roll dough scraps into one 5mm-thick piece; cut out trees and chimney.

4 While shapes are still warm and soft, use tip of sharp knife to cut out small windows from side walls of house, then cut out door from front wall; reserve cut-out door piece. Trim shapes to straighten sides; transfer all shapes to wire racks to cool.

5 Make royal icing. Cover board with foil or silver paper.

6 Secure two crossed skewers to back of each roof piece with icing. Allow to dry before assembling house.

7 Assemble house, securing roof and walls together with icing. If possible, stand house several hours or overnight, supporting sides with four cans, so that it is thoroughly dry before decorating. Decorate board around house with remaining icing to resemble fallen snow.

8 Secure door to house with icing; decorate house with lollies, securing with icing. Secure trees to board and chimney to roof with icing. Dust house with a little sifted icing sugar, if desired.

Cut paper patterns for walls and roof of gingerbread house from thin cardboard.

Secure two crossed skewers to the back of each roof piece with royal icing.

Assemble house on board, securing the roof and walls together with royal icing.

SCOTTISH SHORTBREAD

PREPARATION TIME 20 MINUTES (PLUS REFRIGERATION TIME) **COOKING TIME** 40 MINUTES

Shortbread can be made one week ahead and stored in an airtight container.

250g butter, chopped
⅓ cup (75g) caster sugar
¼ cup (35g) rice flour
2¼ cups (335g) plain flour
2 tablespoons white sugar

1 Preheat oven to slow. Lightly grease two oven trays.
2 Beat butter and caster sugar in medium bowl with electric mixer until light and fluffy; stir in sifted flours, in two batches. Knead on floured surface until smooth.
3 Divide mixture in half; shape into two 20cm rounds on prepared trays. Mark each round into eight wedges, prick with fork, pinch edges with fingers. Sprinkle with white sugar.
4 Bake, uncovered, in slow oven about 40 minutes. Stand 5 minutes then, using sharp knife, cut into wedges along marked lines; cool on trays.

makes 16

GOURMET ROCKY ROAD

PREPARATION TIME 20 MINUTES (PLUS REFRIGERATION TIME)

300g toasted marshmallow with
   coconut, chopped coarsely
400g turkish delight,
   chopped coarsely
¼ cup (40g) toasted blanched
   almonds, chopped coarsely
½ cup (75g) toasted
   shelled pistachios
450g white eating
   chocolate, melted

1 Grease two 8cm x 26cm bar
   cake pans; line base and sides
   with baking paper, extending
   paper 5cm above long sides.
2 Combine marshmallow, turkish
   delight and nuts in large bowl.
   Working quickly, stir in chocolate;
   spread mixture into prepared
   pans, push mixture down firmly
   to flatten the top. Refrigerate
   until set then cut as desired.

STAINED-GLASS CHRISTMAS COOKIES

PREPARATION TIME I HOUR (PLUS REFRIGERATION TIME) **COOKING TIME** I HOUR (PLUS COOLING TIME)

1 Preheat oven to moderate. Line two oven trays with baking paper.

2 Beat butter, rind, essence, sugar, egg and the water in small bowl with electric mixer until smooth (do not overbeat). Transfer to large bowl; stir in flour. Knead dough on floured surface until smooth, cover with plastic wrap; refrigerate 30 minutes.

3 Meanwhile, using rolling pin, gently tap wrapped lollies to crush slightly. Unwrap lollies; separate by colour into small bowls.

4 Roll dough between sheets of baking paper until 4mm thick. Cut shapes from dough using medium-sized cookie cutters; use very small cookie cutters to cut out the centre of each cookie.

5 Place cookies on prepared oven trays; bake, uncovered, in moderate oven 5 minutes. Remove trays from oven; fill cut-out centre of each cookie with a different lolly colour. Return to oven for 5 minutes. Cool cookies on oven trays.

makes 36

For a clear stained-glass effect, use a single-colour lolly for each cookie's window. We used sugar-free fruit drops for this recipe.

Use traditional Christmas cutters such as trees, stars, angels, etc, when cutting out the cookie shapes, and smaller versions of the same shapes for the "stained-glass" centre holes.

If you wish, push a small hole near the top of each cookie through which, after the baked cookie has cooled, you can thread a ribbon to transform the cookie into a Christmas tree decoration.

250g butter, softened
2 teaspoons finely grated lemon rind
½ teaspoon almond essence
¾ cup (165g) caster sugar
1 egg
1 tablespoon water
2¼ cups (335g) plain flour
90g individually wrapped sugar-free
  fruit drops, assorted colours

Using a rolling pin, gently tap the wrapped lollies to crush them lightly.

Use small Christmas cutters to cut the centre out of each of the cookies.

Fill cut-out centres of the cookies with as many different lolly colours as possible.

CHRISTMAS NUT TREE

PREPARATION TIME 30 MINUTES (PLUS REFRIGERATION TIME)

Bring out this tree with the coffee, suggesting to your guests that they snap off bits of the branches. Or, for an impressive gift, wrap the whole tree in cellophane and deliver it on the day.

24cm-round covered cake board
500g dark eating chocolate, melted
1 cup (140g) toasted slivered almonds, chopped finely
½ cup (95g) finely chopped dried figs
100g dark eating chocolate, melted, extra
1 brazil nut
2 teaspoons icing sugar mixture

1 Grease four oven trays; line each with baking paper. Mark nine crosses, measuring 7cm, 9cm, 11cm, 13cm, 14cm, 15cm, 16cm, 17cm and 18cm on trays, leaving about 3cm space between each cross. Mark an 18cm cross on cake board.

2 Combine chocolate, almonds and figs in medium bowl. Drop teaspoonfuls of the chocolate mixture along all the marked crosses to make branches; refrigerate several hours or overnight.

3 Drop about a teaspoon of the extra melted chocolate into the centre of the 18cm cross on cake board; position the 18cm branch on top, moving it around until the best position is found.

4 Assemble the remaining eight branches in pairs, starting from the largest remaining branch and finishing with the smallest, using about a teaspoon of the extra melted chocolate in the centre of each crossed pair; refrigerate until set.

5 Secure each pair to the next with a little melted chocolate (if the branches look a little uneven, support them underneath with a match box). Secure brazil nut to centre of smallest branch with remaining melted chocolate; refrigerate until chocolate sets between branches. Store tree in refrigerator until required; dust with sifted icing sugar.

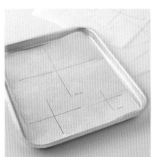
Mark nine crosses on trays, leaving about 3cm space between each cross.

Drop teaspoonfuls of chocolate mixture along all the crosses to make branches.

Assemble branches in pairs, securing one pair to the next with melted chocolate.

WHITE CHOC, LEMON, LIME AND COCONUT

PREPARATION TIME 40 MINUTES
(PLUS REFRIGERATION TIME)
COOKING TIME 5 MINUTES

½ cup (125ml) coconut cream
2 teaspoons finely grated lime rind
2 teaspoons finely grated lemon rind
360g white eating chocolate, chopped coarsely
1¼ cups (85g) shredded coconut

1 Combine coconut cream, rinds and chocolate in small saucepan; stir over low heat until smooth. Transfer mixture to small bowl, cover; refrigerate 3 hours or overnight.
2 Working with a quarter of the chocolate mixture at a time (keeping remainder under refrigeration), roll rounded teaspoons into balls; place on tray. Refrigerate truffles until firm.
3 Working quickly, roll truffles in coconut, return to tray; refrigerate until firm.

makes 30

CRAISIN, PORT AND DARK CHOCOLATE

PREPARATION TIME 40 MINUTES
(PLUS REFRIGERATION TIME)
COOKING TIME 5 MINUTES

¼ cup (60ml) thickened cream
200g dark eating chocolate, chopped coarsely
2 tablespoons port
⅓ cup (50g) craisins, chopped coarsely
300g dark eating chocolate, melted

1 Combine cream and chopped chocolate in small saucepan; stir over low heat until smooth, stir in port and craisins. Transfer to small bowl, cover; refrigerate 3 hours or overnight.
2 Working with a quarter of the chocolate mixture at a time (keeping remainder under refrigeration), roll rounded teaspoons into balls; place on tray. Freeze truffles until firm.
3 Working quickly, dip truffles in melted chocolate then roll gently in hands to coat evenly, return to tray; refrigerate until firm.

makes 30

DARK CHOCOLATE AND GINGER

PREPARATION TIME 40 MINUTES
(PLUS REFRIGERATION TIME)
COOKING TIME 5 MINUTES

⅓ cup (80ml) thickened cream
200g dark eating chocolate, chopped coarsely
½ cup (115g) glacé ginger, chopped finely
¼ cup (25g) cocoa powder

1 Combine cream and chocolate in small saucepan; stir over low heat until smooth, stir in ginger. Transfer to small bowl, cover; refrigerate 3 hours or overnight.
2 Working with a quarter of the chocolate mixture at a time (keeping remainder under refrigeration), roll rounded teaspoons into balls; place on tray. Refrigerate truffles until firm.
3 Working quickly, roll balls in cocoa, return to tray; refrigerate truffles until firm.

makes 30

PEANUT BUTTER AND MILK CHOCOLATE

PREPARATION TIME 40 MINUTES
(PLUS REFRIGERATION TIME)
COOKING TIME 5 MINUTES

⅓ cup (80ml) thickened cream
200g milk eating chocolate, chopped coarsely
¼ cup (70g) unsalted crunchy peanut butter
¾ cup (110g) crushed peanuts

1 Combine cream and chocolate in small saucepan; stir over low heat until smooth, stir in peanut butter. Transfer to small bowl, cover; refrigerate 3 hours or overnight.
2 Working with a quarter of the chocolate mixture at a time (keeping remainder under refrigeration), roll rounded teaspoons into balls; place on tray. Refrigerate truffles until firm.
3 Working quickly, roll balls in peanuts, return to tray; refrigerate truffles until firm.

makes 30

TURKEY

1

Cut off the wing then the hindquarter on the same side, cutting through the thigh bone.

2

Turn the bird on its side; place the cut-off wing and hindquarter under the bird to help keep it steady.

3

Holding the bird firmly with a fork, carve across the breast at top, running along the bird's torso.

4

Carve the leg and wing then turn the bird over and carve the other side in the same manner.

HAM

1

Cut a circle through rind at bone end; run fingers around edge then pull the rind back from the cut.

2

To begin carving, cut a small wedge from the top of the ham close to remaining rind on bone end.

3

Make long sweeps with the knife to get large thin slices. As you carve, the slices will incease in size.

4

As you continue slicing, the ham can be adjusted on the stand so it can be carved from the side.

CHRISTMAS PUDDING

1

Rub about a 40-cm area of flour onto damp hot cloth, leaving flour a little thicker in the centre.

2

Gather cloth evenly around the pudding mixture, avoiding any deep pleats; pat into round shape.

3

Lower pudding into boiling water; tie string ends to handles of the boiler to suspend the pudding.

4

Place a wooden spoon through the knotted loops of the cloth to lift pudding from boiling water.

CHRISTMAS CAKE

1

Line the base and sides of the pan with brown paper, extending paper 5cm above sides of pan.

2

Using your hand, press the cake mixture firmly into the corners of the prepared cake pan.

3

Using a spatula or palette knife, spread the cake mixture to an even thickeness then level the top.

4

The cake is cooked when an inserted knife comes out with no trace of moist mixture on its blade.

GLOSSARY

ALMONDS pointy-ended flat nuts with pitted brown shell enclosing a creamy white kernel that is covered by a brown skin.
blanched brown skins removed.
essence interchangeable with extract; made with almond oil and alcohol or another agent.
slivered small pieces cut lengthways.

ANGOSTURA BITTERS a concentrated food and drink flavouring made from a blend of, reportedly, 40 different herbs and spices. Used in aperitifs, cocktails and digestifs.

BACON RASHERS also known as bacon slices.

BAKING POWDER a raising agent consisting of two parts cream of tartar to one part bicarbonate of soda (baking soda). The acid/alkaline combination, when moistened and heated, gives off carbon dioxide, which aerates and lightens the mixture during baking.

BICARBONATE OF SODA also known as baking soda.

BRIOCHE rich, French yeast-risen bread made with butter and eggs. Available from pâtisseries or specialty bread shops.

BUTTER use salted or unsalted ("sweet") butter; 125g is equal to 1 stick of butter.

CACHOUS small, round cake-decorating sweets available in silver, gold or various colours.

CAPSICUM also known as bell pepper or, simply, pepper. May be coloured red, green, yellow, orange or purplish black. Seeds and membranes should be discarded before use.

CHEESE
bocconcini walnut-sized, fresh baby mozzarella; a delicate, semi-soft, white cheese traditionally made in Italy from buffalo milk. Spoils rapidly, so must be kept under refrigeration, in brine, for only one or two days.
cream commonly known as Philadelphia or Philly; a soft cows-milk cheese with a fat content of at least 33%. Also available as spreadable light cream cheese with a fat content of 21%.
fetta a crumbly goat- or sheep-milk cheese with a sharp salty taste.
goat made from goat milk, has an earthy, strong taste; available in soft and firm textures, in various shapes and sizes, and is sometimes rolled in ash or herbs.
haloumi a firm, sheep-milk cheese matured in brine; cream-coloured, and has a somewhat minty, salty, fetta flavour. Haloumi can be grilled or fried, briefly, without breaking down.
mascarpone a cultured cream product made in much the same way as yogurt. It's whitish to creamy yellow in colour, with a soft, creamy texture.
raclette a melting cheese made from pasteurised cows milk. Has a semi-soft interior dotted with small holes and a rosy, inedible rind. Traditionally melted, raclette has a smooth, creamy taste.

CHILLIES generally the smaller the chilli, the hotter it is. Use rubber gloves when seeding and chopping fresh chillies to prevent burning your skin.
flakes deep-red in colour; dehydrated, extremely fine slices and whole seeds; good for cooking or for sprinkling over cooked food.
thai red also known as "scuds"; small, medium hot, and bright red in colour.

CHORIZO a sausage of Spanish origin, made of coarsely ground pork and highly seasoned with garlic and chillies.

CHOCOLATE MELTS discs of compounded milk, dark or white chocolate. They are good for both melting and moulding.

CINNAMON dried inner bark of the shoots of the cinnamon tree.

CLOVES dried flower buds of a tropical tree; used whole or in ground form.

COINTREAU liqueur with citrus flavouring.

CORIANDER also known as cilantro or chinese parsley. Also sold as seeds, whole or ground.

COULIS originally a French culinary term for the juices that flow into a pan from cooking meat, today it describes a thick puree or sauce made from fruits.

COUSCOUS a fine, grain-like cereal product, originally from North Africa; made from semolina.

CORNFLOUR also known as cornstarch; used as a thickening agent in cooking.

CORNICHONS French for gherkin, a very small variety of cucumber.

CRAISINS dried cranberries.

EGG some recipes in this book call for raw or barely cooked eggs; exercise caution if there is a salmonella problem in your area.

EGGPLANT also known as aubergine. Ranging in size from tiny to very large, and in colour from pale-green to deep-purple. Can also be purchased char-grilled in jars.

ENDIVE, CURLY also known as frisée; a curly-leafed green vegetable, mainly used in salads.

FLOUR
plain an all-purpose flour, made from wheat.
rice extremely fine flour made from ground rice.
self-raising plain flour sifted with baking powder in the proportion of 1 cup flour to 2 teaspoons baking powder.

GELATINE we used powdered gelatine; also available in sheet form, known as leaf gelatine.

GINGER we used freshly grated fresh ginger unless specified differently. Also known as green or root ginger, this spice comes from the thick root of a tropical plant.

glacé fresh ginger root preserved in sugar syrup. Crystallised ginger can be substituted if rinsed with warm water and dried before using.
ground also known as powdered ginger; used as a flavouring in cakes, pies and puddings. Cannot be substituted for fresh ginger.

GOLDEN SYRUP a by-product of refined sugarcane; pure maple syrup or honey can be substituted.

HARISSA Moroccan sauce or paste made from dried red chillies, garlic, oil and sometimes caraway seeds.

ICE-CREAM use a good quality ice-cream; actual varieties of ice-cream differ from manufacturer to manufacturer depending on the quantities of air and fat that have been incorporated into the mixture.

JAM also known as preserve or conserve; most often made from fruit.

KAFFIR LIME LEAVES aromatic leaves of a citrus tree; used similarly to bay leaves, especially in Thai cooking. A strip of fresh lime peel may be substituted for each kaffir lime leaf.

KECAP MANIS also known as ketjap manis, or sieu wan. A dark, thick, sweet soy sauce with added sugar and spices. Used in most South-East Asian cuisines.

KIPFLER POTATO small, finger-shaped potato with a nutty flavour; great baked and in salads.

KUMARA orange-fleshed sweet potato often confused with yam.

LAMINGTON PAN 20cm x 30cm slab cake pan, 3cm deep.

LOLLIES small candies and confectionery.

LYCHEES delicious fresh fruit with a light texture and flavour; peel away rough skin, remove seed and use. Also available in cans.

MINCE MEAT also known as ground meat.

MIRIN sweet rice wine used in Japanese cooking; not to be confused with sake.

MIXED PEEL candied citrus peel.

MIXED SPICE a blend of ground spices usually consisting of cinnamon, allspice and nutmeg.

MIZUNA LEAVES originally from Japan, a feathery green salad leaf that's sharp in flavour.

PARSLEY, FLAT-LEAF also known as continental parsley or italian parsley.

PASTRY, READY-ROLLED PUFF packaged sheets of frozen puff pastry available from supermarkets.

PANCETTA cured pork belly; substitute with bacon.

PEPITAS dried pumpkin seeds; used in cooking or eaten as a snack.

PEPPERCORNS
sichuan also known as szechuan or chinese pepper, native to the Sichuan province of China. A mildly hot spice with a distinctive peppery-lemon flavour and aroma.
black is picked when the berry is not quite ripe, then dried until it shrivels and the skin turns dark brown to black. It's the strongest flavoured of all the peppercorn varieties.

POLENTA a flour-like cereal made of ground corn (maize); similar to cornmeal but coarser and darker. Also the name of the dish made from it.

POMEGRANATE MOLASSES not to be confused with pomegranate syrup or grenadine (a sweet red liquid used in cocktails); pomegranate molasses is thicker, browner and more concentrated in flavour, having similar qualities to balsamic vinegar, nicely tart and sharp, slightly sweet and fruity. Pomegranate molasses is available at Middle-Eastern food stores and specialty food shops.

PROSCIUTTO cured, air-dried, pressed ham.

RAMBUTANS similar in size to a lychee, this dark crimson tropical fruit is covered with hairy tentacles; inside the shell is the edible part, a sweet, crisp, off-white juicy fruit having a small centre seed which is to be discarded.

RICE PAPER SHEETS also known as banh trang. Made from rice paste and stamped into rounds; stores well at room temperature. Are quite brittle and will break if dropped; dipped momentarily in water become pliable wrappers for fried food and uncooked vegetables. Make good spring-roll wrappers.

RICE STICK NOODLES popular South-East Asian dried rice noodle. Come in different widths, thin used in soups, wide in stir-fries, but all should be soaked in hot water until soft.

SHALLOTS also called french shallots, golden shallots or eschalots; small, elongated, brown-skinned members of the onion family. Grows in tight clusters similar to garlic.

SPATCHCOCK a small chicken (poussin), no more than 6 weeks old, weighing a maximum 500g. Also, a cooking technique where a small chicken is split open, then flattened and grilled.

STAR ANISE a dried star-shaped fruit of a tree native to China. The pods, which have an astringent aniseed or liquorice flavour, are widely used in the Asian kitchen. Available whole and ground.

STAR FRUIT also known as carambola, five-corner fruit or chinese star fruit; pale green or yellow colour. It has a clean, crisp texture; flavour may be either sweet or sour, depending on variety and when picked. There is no need to peel or seed it, and they're slow to discolour. Avoid any with brown specks or streaks.

STOCK available in cans, bottles or tetra packs. Stock cubes or powder can be used.

SUGAR we used coarse, granulated table sugar, also known as crystal sugar, unless otherwise specified.
brown an extremely soft, fine granulated sugar retaining molasses for its characteristic colour and flavour. Dark brown sugar may be substituted.
caster also known as superfine or finely granulated table sugar.
icing sugar mixture also known as confectioners' sugar or powdered sugar.
palm made from the sap of the sugar palm tree. Light brown to black in colour and usually sold in rock-hard cakes; substitute it with brown sugar if unavailable.
pure icing also known as confectioners' sugar or powdered sugar.

SULTANAS also known as golden raisins; dried seedless white grapes.

SWEETENED CONDENSED MILK from which 60% of the water has been removed; the remaining milk is then sweetened with sugar.

TOMATO
cherry also known as Tiny Tim or Tom Thumb tomatoes; small and round.
egg also called plum or Roma; these are smallish and oval-shaped.
sun-dried we used packaged sun-dried tomatoes in oil, unless otherwise specified.
truss small vine-ripened tomatoes with vine still attached.

TREACLE thick, dark syrup not unlike molasses; a by-product of sugar refining.

TURKEY BUFFE an unboned whole turkey breast with wings attached.

TURKISH DELIGHT also known as lokum; made in Turkey, it is a unique sweet concoction of sugar syrup, various flavourings, nuts and dried fruit.

VANILLA BEAN dried long, thin pod from a tropical golden orchid grown in Central and South America and Tahiti; the minuscule black seeds inside the bean are used to impart a luscious vanilla flavour in baking and desserts. A whole bean can be placed in the sugar container to make the vanilla sugar often called for in recipes.

VIETNAMESE MINT not a mint at all, but a pungent, peppery narrow-leafed member of the buckwheat family. It is a common ingredient in Thai cooking.

VINEGAR
balsamic made from white Trebbiano grapes specially processed then aged in antique wooden casks to give an exquisite pungent flavour.
cider (apple cider) made from fermented apples.
raspberry made from fresh raspberries steeped in a white wine vinegar.
red wine based on fermented red wine.
sherry natural vinegar aged in oak according to the traditional Spanish system; a mellow wine vinegar named for its colour.
white wine made from white wine.
rice wine made from rice wine lees (sediment), salt and alcohol.

WASABI a Japanese horseradish used to make the green-coloured, pungent sauce traditionally served with Japanese raw fish dishes; sold in powdered or paste form.

WITLOF also known as chicory or belgian endive.

WONTON WRAPPERS gow gee, egg or spring roll pastry sheets can be substituted. Store them in the refrigerator or freezer, but let them come to room temperature before using.

ZUCCHINI also known as courgette; a small green, yellow or white vegetable that belongs to the squash family.

INDEX

Asian fruit salad 73
asian-spiced
  barbecued turkey 31
Asian-style baked ham 32
asparagus with parmesan,
  pan-fried 21
Aussie barbecued ham 35
Australian iced tea 5
balsamic-glazed
  baby onions 58
basic fruit mixture 82
beef fillet with horseradish
  cream sauce 40
beef with mustard 13
beetroots with caper
  vinaigrette, baby 63
bellini 6
berry punch, mixed 7
bocconcini, marinated 20
boiled Christmas pudding 94
broccolini polonaise 60
cake
  celebration fruit 92
  festive fruit and nut 90
  pudding, frozen
    chocolate fruit 101
  ginger and lime 70
  grand marnier fruit 86
  irish pudding 98
  last-minute fruit 93
  moist Christmas 84
caperberries with
  warm potato salad 61
capsicum, barbecued corn
  and broad beans 62
carrot, parsnip and
  roasted pumpkin,
  middle-eastern 52
carrots with orange
  maple syrup, baby 58
champagne cocktail 4
cheesecake, fruit
  cake 'n' eggnog 77
chicken coconut salad
  in crisp wonton cups 23
chocolate fruit cake
  pudding, frozen 101
chocolate tart, gourmet 72
chocolate, white, and
  pistachio parfait 75
Christmas
  cake cream parfaits 69
  cake ice-cream terrine 69
  cake, moist 84
  cookies, stained glass 107
  nut tree 108
  pudding 82
  pudding, boiled 94
  pudding, steamed 88
citrus and glacé fruit
  frozen puddings with
  bitter orange sauce 89
cocktail, champagne 4
cookies, stained-glass
  Christmas 107
coriander and seafood
  salad, chilli-marinated 51
corn, barbecued, broad
  beans and capsicum 62

crab rice paper rolls 15
crepe cakes, salmon
  and dilled sour cream 19
crostini, duck and hoisin 13
daiquiri, mango 5
drunken watermelon 6
duck and hoisin crostini 13
egg and ham slice 67
endive, lychee and
  papaya salad with
  passionfruit dressing 65
fetta and fig 12
fetta, tomato and leek
  tartlets, marinated 8
fig and fetta 12
frittata, pumpkin
  and spinach 21
fruit and nut cake 90
fruit cake 'n' eggnog
  cheesecake 77
fruit cake, celebration 92
fruit cake, frozen
  chocolate pudding 101
fruit cake, grand marnier 86
fruit cake, last-minute 93
fruit mince slice 85
fruit salad, Asian 73
ginger and lime cake 70
gingerbread house 102
glacé fruit and citrus
  frozen puddings with
  bitter orange sauce 89
glacé fruit slice with
  limoncello cream 97
goat cheese and
  roasted vegie tart 68
grand marnier fruit cake 86
gravlax, vodka-cured 12
green salad with orange
  vinaigrette 56
haloumi, prosciutto
  and spinach salad 57
ham and egg slice 67
ham, Asian-style baked 32
ham, Aussie barbecued 35
ice-cream and Christmas
  cake terrine 69
iced tea, Australian 5
irish pudding cake 98
kebabs, mini scallop
  and lime 11
kumara, roasted, mustard
  and honey-glaze 55
leek, tomato and
  marinated fetta tartlets 8
leeks in vinaigrette 59
lemon lime sorbet 81
lime and ginger cake 70
lime and mint spritzer 7
lychee, endive and
  papaya salad with
  passionfruit dressing 65
mango daiquiri 5
mustard and honey-glazed
  roasted kumara 55
mixed berry punch 7
nut tree, Christmas 108
onions, balsamic-glazed
  baby 58

oysters
  with chive béchamel 17
  with lime and wasabi 16
  with red wine vinegar 16
  with sauce cuore 17
papaya, endive and lychee
  salad with passionfruit
  dressing 65
parfait, white chocolate
  and pistachio 75
parfaits, Christmas
  cake cream 69
passionfruit curd tartlets 78
passionfruit sorbet 81
pavlova, very-berry 76
pea, salmon and
  mint bavette 67
peas, fresh, caraway
  and parmesan 59
peanut butter and milk
  chocolate truffles 111
pistachio and white
  chocolate parfait 75
pomegranate-glazed
  turkey with cornbread
  seasoning 27
pork loin with spinach
  and pancetta stuffing 36
pork neck, barbecued 39
potato
  barbecued kipflers 55
  mediterranean mash 54
  salad with caperberries,
  warm 61
  perfect roast 54
poultry platter 43
prawns, slow-cooked
  spicy herbed 18
prawns, spicy 20
prosciutto and raclette
  parcels in vine leaves 10
prosciutto, haloumi
  and spinach salad 57
pudding
  irish, cake 98
  boiled Christmas 94
  Christmas 82
  frozen chocolate
  fruit cake 101
  steamed Christmas 88
puddings, glacé fruit and
  citrus with bitter orange
  sauce, frozen 89
pumpkin and
  spinach frittata 21
pumpkin, carrot and
  parsnip, middle-eastern
  roasted 0.52
punch, mixed berry 7
punch, party 4
raclette parcels in vine
  leaves and prosciutto 10
raspberry sorbet 81
rice noodle salad with
  wasabi dressing 64
rice paper rolls, crab 15
rocky road, gourmet 105
salmon, pea and
  mint bavette 67

salmon, slow-roasted
  with pesto 47
salmon and dilled sour
  cream crepe cakes 19
scallop and lime kebabs 11
seafood platter, cold 48
seafood salad, coriander
  and chilli-marinated 51
sesame patty-pan squash
  and sugar snap peas 62
shortbread, scottish 104
slice, fruit mince 85
slice, glacé fruit, with
  limoncello cream 97
slice, ham and egg 67
sorbet, lemon lime 81
sorbet, passionfruit 81
sorbet, raspberry 81
spinach and
  pumpkin frittata 21
spinach, haloumi and
  prosciutto salad 57
steamed Christmas
  pudding 88
tart, goat cheese and
  roasted vegie 68
tart, gourmet chocolate 72
tartlets, passionfruit curd 78
three-in-one
  Christmas mix 82
tomato, leek and
  marinated fetta tartlets 8
tomatoes with crispy basil
  leaves, roasted truss 63
trout, with thai-flavours
  hollandaise, salt-crusted
  ocean 44
truffles, craisin, port and
  dark chocolate 110
truffles, dark chocolate
  and ginger 111
truffles, peanut butter
  and milk chocolate 111
truffles white choc, lemon,
  lime and coconut 110
turkey
  barbecued with
  asian spices 31
  buffé with couscous
  stuffing 28
  with pomegranate
  glaze and cornbread
  seasoning 27
  rillettes 66
  salad sandwiches 68
  salad, vietnamese 66
  with forcemeat stuffing,
  traditional 24
vegetable and goat
  cheese terrine, roasted 22
vine leaves parcels with
  raclette and prosciutto 10
watermelon, drunken 6
white choc, lemon, lime
  and coconut truffles 110
white chocolate and
  pistachio parfait 75
yabbies with remoulade
  on baguette 14

FACTS & FIGURES

Wherever you live, you'll be able to use our recipes with the help of these easy-to-follow conversions. While these conversions are approximate only, the difference between an exact and the approximate conversion of various liquid and dry measures is but minimal, and will not affect your cooking results.

liquid measures

metric	imperial
30ml	1 fluid oz
60ml	2 fluid oz
100ml	3 fluid oz
125ml	4 fluid oz
150ml	5 fluid oz (¼ pint/1 gill)
190ml	6 fluid oz
250ml	8 fluid oz
300ml	10 fluid oz (½ pint)
500ml	16 fluid oz
600ml	20 fluid oz (1 pint)
1000ml (1 litre)	1¾ pints

dry measures

metric	imperial
15g	½oz
30g	1oz
60g	2oz
90g	3oz
125g	4oz (¼lb)
155g	5oz
185g	6oz
220g	7oz
250g	8oz (½lb)
280g	9oz
315g	10oz
345g	11oz
375g	12oz (¾lb)
410g	13oz
440g	14oz
470g	15oz
500g	16oz (1lb)
750g	24oz (1½lb)
1kg	32oz (2lb)

helpful measures

metric	imperial
3mm	⅛in
6mm	¼in
1cm	½in
2cm	¾in
2.5cm	1in
5cm	2in
6cm	2½in
8cm	3in
10cm	4in
13cm	5in
15cm	6in
18cm	7in
20cm	8in
23cm	9in
25cm	10in
28cm	11in
30cm	12in (1ft)

measuring equipment

The difference between one country's measuring cups and another's is, at most, within a 2 or 3 teaspoon variance. (For the record, one Australian metric measuring cup holds approximately 250ml.) The most accurate way of measuring dry ingredients is to weigh them. When measuring liquids, use a clear glass or plastic jug with metric markings. (One Australian metric tablespoon holds 20ml; one Australian metric teaspoon holds 5ml.)

how to measure

When using graduated metric measuring cups, shake dry ingredients loosely into the appropriate cup. Do not tap the cup on a bench or tightly pack the ingredients unless directed to do so. Level top of measuring cups and measuring spoons with a knife. When measuring liquids, place a clear glass or plastic jug with metric markings on a flat surface to check accuracy at eye level.

Note: North America, NZ and the UK use 15ml tablespoons. All cup and spoon measurements are level.

We use large eggs having an average weight of 60g.

oven temperatures

These oven temperatures are only a guide. Always check the manufacturer's manual.

	°C (Celsius)	°F (Fahrenheit)	Gas Mark
Very slow	120	250	½
Slow	140 – 150	275 – 300	1 – 2
Moderately slow	170	325	3
Moderate	180 – 190	350 – 375	4 – 5
Moderately hot	200	400	6
Hot	220 – 230	425 – 450	7 – 8
Very hot	240	475	9

ARE YOU MISSING SOME OF THE WORLD'S FAVOURITE COOKBOOKS?

The Australian Women's Weekly Cookbooks are available from bookshops, cookshops, supermarkets and other stores all over the world. You can also buy direct from the publisher, using the order form below.

TITLE	RRP	QTY
Almost Vegetarian	£5.99	
Asian, Meals in Minutes	£5.99	
Babies & Toddlers Good Food	£5.99	
Barbecue Meals In Minutes	£5.99	
Basic Cooking Class	£5.99	
Beginners Cooking Class	£5.99	
Beginners Simple Meals	£5.99	
Beginners Thai	£5.99	
Best Ever Slimmers' Recipes	£5.99	
Best Food	£5.99	
Best Food Desserts	£5.99	
Best Food Fast	£5.99	
Best Food Mains	£5.99	
Cakes Cooking Class	£5.99	
Caribbean Cooking	£5.99	
Casseroles	£5.99	
Chicken Meals in Minutes	£5.99	
Chinese Cooking Class	£5.99	
Christmas Cooking	£5.99	
Cocktails	£5.99	
Cooking for Friends	£5.99	
Creative Cooking on a Budget	£5.99	
Detox (Sept 05)	£5.99	
Dinner Beef	£5.99	
Dinner Lamb (Aug 05)	£5.99	
Dinner Seafood	£5.99	
Easy Australian Style	£5.99	
Easy Curry	£5.99	
Easy Spanish-Style	£5.99	
Essential Soup	£5.99	
Freezer, Meals from the	£5.99	
French Cooking Class	£5.99	
French Food, New	£5.99	
Fresh Food for Babies & Toddlers	£5.99	
Get Real, Make a Meal	£5.99	

TITLE	RRP	QTY
Good Food Fast	£5.99	
Great Lamb Cookbook	£5.99	
Greek Cooking Class	£5.99	
Healthy Heart Cookbook	£5.99	
Indian Cooking Class	£5.99	
Japanese Cooking Class	£5.99	
Kids' Birthday Cakes	£5.99	
Kids Cooking	£5.99	
Lean Food	£5.99	
Low-carb, Low-fat	£5.99	
Low-fat Feasts	£5.99	
Low-fat Food For Life	£5.99	
Low-fat Meals in Minutes	£5.99	
Main Course Salads	£5.99	
Middle Eastern Cooking Class	£5.99	
Midweek Meals in Minutes	£5.99	
Muffins, Scones & Breads	£5.99	
New Casseroles	£5.99	
New Classics	£5.99	
New Finger Food	£5.99	
Party Food and Drink (Oct 05)	£5.99	
Pasta Meals in Minutes	£5.99	
Potatoes	£5.99	
Quick Meals in Minutes	£5.99	
Salads: Simple, Fast & Fresh	£5.99	
Saucery	£5.99	
Sensational Stir-Fries	£5.99	
Short-order Cook	£5.99	
Slim	£5.99	
Sweet Old Fashioned Favourites	£5.99	
Thai Cooking Class	£5.99	
Vegetarian Meals in Minutes	£5.99	
Weekend Cook	£5.99	
Wicked Sweet Indulgences	£5.99	
Wok, Meals in Minutes	£5.99	
TOTAL COST:	**£**	

NAME

ADDRESS

POSTCODE

DAYTIME PHONE

I ENCLOSE MY CHEQUE/MONEY ORDER FOR £

OR PLEASE CHARGE MY VISA, ACCESS OR MASTERCARD NUMBER

CARD HOLDER'S NAME

EXPIRY DATE

CARDHOLDER'S SIGNATURE

To order: Mail or fax – photocopy or complete the order form above, and send your credit card details or cheque payable to: Australian Consolidated Press (UK), Moulton Park Business Centre, Red House Road, Moulton Park, Northampton NN3 6AQ, phone (+44) (0) 1604 497531, fax (+44) (0) 1604 497533, e-mail books@acpuk.com Or order online at www.acpuk.com

Non-UK residents: We accept the credit cards listed on the coupon, or cheques, drafts or International Money Orders payable in sterling and drawn on a UK bank. Credit card charges are at the exchange rate current at the time of payment.

Postage and packing UK: Add £1.00 per order plus 50p per book.

Postage and packing overseas: Add £2.00 per order plus £1.00 per book.

Offer ends 31.12.2005

Test Kitchen
Food director *Pamela Clark*
Food editor *Karen Hammial*
Assistant food editor *Amira Georgy*
Test Kitchen manager *Cathie Lonnie*
Home economists *Sammie Coryton, Nancy Duran, Benjamin Haslam, Elizabeth Macri, Christina Martignago, Sharon Reeve, Susie Riggall, Kirrily Smith, Vanessa Vetter*
Editorial coordinator *Rebecca Steyns*

ACP Books
Editorial director *Susan Tomnay*
Creative director *Hieu Chi Nguyen*
Senior editor *Wendy Bryant*
Designer *Caryl Wiggins*
Studio manager *Caryl Wiggins*
Editorial assistant *Merryn Pearse*
Sales director *Brian Cearnes*
Rights manager *Jane Hazell*
Brand manager *Renée Crea*
Sales & marketing coordinator *Gabrielle Botto*
Pre-press *Harry Palmer*
Production manager *Carol Currie*
Business manager *Seymour Cohen*
Business analyst *Marena Paul*
Chief executive officer *John Alexander*
Group publisher *Pat Ingram*
Publisher *Sue Wannan*
Editor-in-chief *Deborah Thomas*

Produced by ACP Books, Sydney.
Printed by Dai Nippon Printing in Korea.
Published by ACP Publishing Pty Limited, 54 Park St, Sydney; GPO Box 4088, Sydney, NSW 2001.
Ph: (02) 9282 8618 Fax: (02) 9267 9438.
acpbooks@acp.com.au
www.acpbooks.com.au
To order books, phone 136 116.
Send recipe enquiries to:
recipeenquiries@acp.com.au
AUSTRALIA: Distributed by Network Services, GPO Box 4088, Sydney, NSW 2001.
Ph: (02) 9282 8777 Fax: (02) 9264 3278.
UNITED KINGDOM: Distributed by Australian Consolidated Press (UK), Moulton Park Business Centre, Red House Rd, Moulton Park, Northampton, NN3 6AQ.
Ph: (01604) 497 531 Fax: (01604) 497 533
acpukltd@aol.com
CANADA: Distributed by Whitecap Books Ltd, 351 Lynn Ave, North Vancouver, BC, V7J 2C4.
Ph: (604) 980 9852 Fax: (604) 980 8197
customerservice@whitecap.ca
www.whitecap.ca
NEW ZEALAND: Distributed by Netlink Distribution Company, ACP Media Centre, Cnr Fanshawe and Beaumont Streets, Westhaven, Auckland.
PO Box 47906, Ponsonby, Auckland, NZ.
Ph: (09) 366 9966 ask@ndcnz.co.nz
SOUTH AFRICA: Distributed by PSD Promotions (Pty) Ltd, PO Box 1175, Isando, 1600, Gauteng, Johannesburg, SA.
Ph: (011) 392 6065 Fax (011) 392 6079
orders@psdprom.co.za

Clark, Pamela.
The Australian Women's Weekly Christmas Cooking.
Includes index.
ISBN 1 86396 370 7
1. Christmas cookery. I. Title.
II Title: Australian Women's Weekly
641.5686
© ACP Publishing Pty Limited 2004
ABN 18 053 273 546
This publication is copyright. No part of it may be reproduced or transmitted in any form without the written permission of the publishers.
First published 2004. Reprinted 2005.
The publishers would like to thank the following for props used in photography:
Arte Flowers, Woollahra
Atmosphere Concepts, Surry Hills
Beach House Collections, Avalon
Bison Homewares, www.bisonhome.com
Chee Soon Fitzgerald, Surry Hills
Country Road Homewares
Design Mode International, Mona Vale
House @ Warringah Mall, Brookvale
Mud Australia, Marrickville
Storehouse Homewares, Brookvale
Village Living, Avalon
Wheel & Barrow, Chatswood